lead yourself

WHO'S
YO

STEERING UR BOAT?

lead yourself

be where others will follow

Mick Cope

PERSEUS
PUBLISHING

A Member of the
Perseus Books Group

www.yourmomentum.com/leadyourself

the stuff that drives you

What is momentum?

Momentum is a completely new publishing philosophy, in print and online, dedicated to giving you more of the information, inspiration and drive to enhance who you are, what you do, and how you do it.

Fusing the changing forces of work, life and technology, momentum will give you the bright stuff for a brighter future and set you on the way to being all you can be.

Who needs momentum?

Momentum is for people who want to make things happen in their career and their life, who want to work at something they enjoy and that's worthy of their talent and their time. Momentum people have values and principles, and question who they are, what they do, and who for. Wherever they work, they want to feel proud of what they do. And they are hungry for information, stimulation, ideas and answers.

Momentum online

Visit *www.yourmomentum.com* to be part of the talent community. Here you'll find a fully listing of current and future books, an archive of articles by momentum authors, sample chapters and self-assessment tools. While you're there, post your work/life questions to our momentum coaches and sign up to receive free newsletters with even more stuff to drive you.

For two people who helped me start my personal leadership journey

Paul Oliver
Ed Percival

For information on the *Lead Yourself* development programmes please visit:

www.WizOz.co.uk

You can also contact Mick Cope at Mick@WizOz.co.uk

First printing, August 2002

1 2 3 4 5 6 7 8 9 10—06 05 04 03 02

Library of Congress Cataloging-in-Publication Data is available.
ISBN 0-7382-0653-9

Perseus Publishing is a Member of the Perseus Books Group.

Find us on the World Wide Web at
http://www.perseuspublishing.com

Perseus Publishing books are available at special discounts for bulk purchases in the U.S. by corporations, institutions, and other organizations. For more information, please contact the Special Markets Department at the Perseus Books Group, 11 Cambridge Center, Cambridge, MA 02142, or call (800) 255-1514 or (617)252-5298, or e-mail j.mccrary@perseusbooks.com.

Copyright © Pearson Education Limited 2001

This edition of *Lead Yourself* First Edition is published by arrangement with Pearson Education Limited

Text design by Heat and Sue Lamble Book Design

thank you...

to Paul Oliver for the original inspiration

to Sara Rowe and Dave Chitty for helping to develop the original themes and ideas

and to my editor, Rachael Stock, for her feedback and help in enhancing the manuscript

also, to Jacqueline Cassidy for her work on editing the book

a big hug to Lin for letting me write on holiday

and Lucy, Matt and Mike for putting up with my moods

thanks to Marie Humphreys, Catherine Action, Francesca Corletti and

Andy McClarron for helping the programme take its first few steps

to Gary Porter for co-creating the *Lead Yourself* CD single – free copies available

from mick@wizoz.co.uk

opening

Personal leadership

heart
take control of your rudder

Decision 1 choose your choice

Decision 2 know where you're going

head
enlarging the map

hand
leadership in action

closing

Your choice now...

figures

personal leadership

We live in a world that faces unseen changes. Within organizations, we see managers struggling to come to terms with new demands on their managerial and leadership style. We have shifted from a position where control is managed by virtue of a formal badge of office (manager, parent, director etc.) to one where we have to lead people through the use of more intangible and flexible forms of leadership.

People are no longer prepared to accept the 'do what I say' regime, they respond to a 'do what I do' leadership style.

If we are to lead ourselves and others more effectively, we have to get serious about the idea of personal leadership rather than plastic leadership. To achieve this, the personal leadership framework offered in this book challenges you to consider how you currently lead yourself and others against three key aspects.

This is leadership where the whole you is aligned, centred and able to build relationships with anyone you live or work with.

◆ **Leadership drivers** – the deep inner forces that help and hinder our personal leadership style. They have a major impact on where we get our personal security from, the level of variety with which we view the world, and our ability to build trusting relationships.

◆ **Leadership dimensions** – the visible manifestations of our leadership style. We all have a leadership style that consists of three dimensions: how we feel, think and behave. Some of us are dominant in one or have a deficit in another. The essence of personal leadership is to manage the balance between these three factors and to work towards a greater degree of alignment.

◆ **Leadership decisions** – the decisions that determine how we lead others and ourselves. We all have to make choices, define where we are going, map the world, manage change, understand others and share success. If we don't make these choices, someone else will make them for us.

This book isn't an exercise in finding fault with your current leadership style, but it will help you discover how you could be different and how to shift the way you feel, think and behave.

Personal leadership drivers

At the heart of personal leadership capability are three drivers (see Figure 1). These drivers are the energy that helps us be successful, or

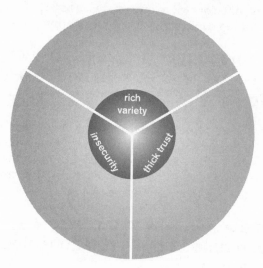

Figure 1 *Leadership drivers*

the inner voice that spurs us on. But they can also manifest themselves as procrastination or as our inner critic. The first step in leading yourself is to understand the three drivers, discover how they influence you and choose what role they play in your new personal leadership style.

- **Insecurity versus *in*-security** – ever feel you're not good enough, powerful enough or rich enough? That feeling that you can't do something is generally a figment of your imagination, manufactured by you. Its driver is routed in the curse of insecurity, the sense that you're not good enough to do things that others believe you capable of; as a result you draw your personal power from external validation – like job titles and badges of office. The personal leadership framework will show you a way to manage and reduce this, giving you the power to fulfill your promise. This kind of living and leading is driven by *in*-security, where your personal energy comes from within rather than from outside.

- **Restricted variety versus rich variety** – as the world becomes more and more complex, we must respond with increasing originality, diversity and richness. Often our thoughts are stifled, but by broadening our view of the world, we create more choices, and operate from the perspective of rich variety, using a personal map that offers us a multitude of options and choices.

- **Thin trust versus thick trust** – in an ever more fragmented and disparate world, we rely increasingly on our ability to build and maintain successful relationships. Every time we meet or interact with someone, face to face, or by mail or e-mail, we draw on one single question to determine if the relationship will work: can I trust this person? No longer is trust a soft variable, it's now the hard factor that binds commercial and caring relationships in a world that is disentangling at Internet speed. Thin relationships are those grounded in only partial or limited trust, whereas thick relationships are solid and lasting.

The importance of ensuring that your three drivers are *in*-security, rich variety and thick trust can't be underestimated. Just think about the last time you read a personal development book, attended a training course or made a decision to improve a certain part of your life. Remember early promises, full of excitement and focus? They soon turn into pockets empty of improvement once you hit reality. Change isn't quite so easy as you thought it might be. Failure to realize planned personal improvement is usually one of several types:

◆ Once faced with a personal challenge in the area you want to improve, the little inner voice kicks in and challenges your assumptions. Insecurity whispers in your ear: 'are you really ready to give up smoking?'; 'do you really think that this time-management tool will help?'; 'you're not as good as those people, what makes you think that you can tell them what to do?'

◆ Back from the personal development course all fired up with a new set of ideas and goals, you find they collapse in a heap once you try to use them. The problem is that you're trying to implement a new set of ideals using a redundant map of the world. You're still operating with your old, restricted vision and haven't thought about how to introduce a richer variety into the way you lead yourself.

◆ You've learnt new ways of thinking, watched the video on how to build relationships and listened to the guru telling you their innermost secrets that helped them make a million. But when you go back to the workplace and try to effect a change, you're still operating on relationships precariously balanced on thin trust. Before you can make any change in your relationships you must understand how to build and maintain thick trust. Without this, all the new positive-thinking techniques will be just that, positive thinking without positive action.

Enhanced personal leadership isn't something you get from the back of a cereal box or off a bookshelf. This book will help you think about how you might make improvements but, at the end of the day, deep restraining forces inhibit our ability to make effective and sustainable change. Unless you become aware of these drivers and how to manage them, it will be tough to realize any improvements in the way you lead yourself and others.

Personal leadership dimensions

How we lead ourselves and others is determined by three dimensions – the head, heart and hand (see Figure 2) – which dictate the way we think, feel and behave.

◆ **Heart.** This is the emotional epicenter that provides the inner strength and compass of leaders, regulating the desire and ability to make choices about important things in our lives and giving us

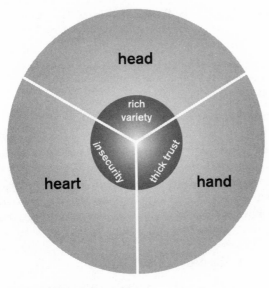

Figure 2 *Heart, head and hand dimensions*

direction. When both these aspects are effective, we can make tough choices with a clear sense of purpose. When less effective, we avoid making decisions and, when we do, they are driven by other people's goals rather than an inner purpose.

Think of people who have climbed the corporate ladder only to find they are found wanting when they are required to make tough decisions that will determine the direction the company takes in its next venture. An amazing intellect coupled with the ability to manage relationships can be used to good end in the corporate jungle, but it can be easy to simply surf the wave of success. So many rising stars, future business leaders, flounder once they reach a position where they have to set direction and make strategic decisions.

◆ **Head.** This dimension provides the wisdom and clarity of purpose that can regulate the excesses of an emotional heart. The head function remains above our emotional needs and helps us formulate plans and make decisions relating to how we lead ourselves and others. Effective head orientation will produce a leader who takes a broad, aerial view of life and who has, as a result, a rich and varied perspective. They will also be adaptable and able to change how they provide leadership in varying circumstances.

Someone lacking in this dimension will only operate according to their own map of the world, believing it's always 'right'. Leading themselves and others, they will be resolute in the belief that there is only one way to manage change and that their way is best. This lack of reason can have a self-destructive effect in so many people.

◆ **Hand.** Once the heart has set the direction and the head has decided how to move forward, then we take action. Effective leaders exhibit two core behaviours. They are able to step out of the world they operate in into the world of the people they lead. Once they understand the other person's universe they behave in a way that enables all concerned to share in the final outcome. Those lacking in this ability will often try to achieve only their personal goals in the belief that the leader is there to win rather than to collaborate. They will lead in a detached way without understanding the people they are leading.

I know one person who had all the necessary passion and intelligence to become a leading professor in his field. He consistently generated breakthrough concepts and ideas that were quite astounding in their depth and breadth. But when he had to put his ideas across, his inability to connect with others through his relationships resulted in people being unable to associate with his ideas, finding no connection with him as a person. His emotions and intelligence failed to help him build trust-based relationships. His head and heart were strong but the hand dimension failed to help him realize his true personal value.

All three dimensions of heart, head and hand must be constantly in tune and in alignment. When all three are carefully managed, we have someone with a clear sense of personal leadership, able to lead others effectively.

Personal leadership decisions
Once we understand the three drivers and their corresponding dimensions, we can make decisions about our leadership style. The personal leadership framework suggests that, regardless of whether you're a parent, manager, technician or student, there are six core choices that influence how we lead ourselves and others.

Heart decisions

◆ **Choose your choice.** You might believe that you manage choice in your life, but the reality is that we often concede or trade away much of this power to others. Effective personal leadership is dependent on the extent to which we retain the ability to make choices.

◆ **Know where you're going.** There is little point in harnessing the power to make choices unless we know why we are making them. The aim is to define a set of clear personal goals and outcomes to use as criteria by which choices are made.

Head decisions

◆ **Map your map.** Don't just rely on your current map of the world. Constantly seek to discover and understand other people's maps so that you broaden your view and create more options and choices in the way you lead yourself and others.

◆ **Change how you change.** If you do what you always did, you will get what you always got. Your outcome might be clear, but the route to your end goal might offer challenges and barriers that you have never encountered before. For change to be effective and sustainable you need to learn how to manage it using alternative styles.

Hand decisions

◆ **Step inside out.** To effectively deliver personal, sustainable success, you need to understand what success means for other people. To do this you have to step outside your view of the world and into theirs. Only when you understand how others think, feel and behave can you actually understand what success is like for them.

◆ **Share success.** Successful personal leadership is founded on the notion of shared outcomes and sustainable success. Personal leadership that is selfish or short-lived is not truly successful.

The personal leadership framework

The personal leadership structure (Figure 3) isn't designed to offer 'the answer' – only you can lead yourself – but this model pulls together a wide and diverse range of thoughts, ideas and techniques that people have used to achieve a greater degree of control over their lives and improve how they lead others.

Drivers, dimension and decisions all come together to make up the personal leadership framework.

The drivers that condition our behaviour, *in*-security, variety and trust, all create a personal leadership style that can be described in

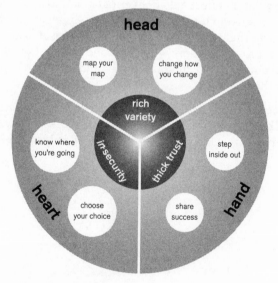

Figure 3 *Personal leadership framework*

Drivers	Dimensions	Decisions
In-security – ignore self-limiting inner voices	**Heart** – drives your direction and purpose	**Choose your choice** – before someone else does it for you
		Know where you're going – so you can make the right decisions today
Rich variety – choose to see the world with more clarity and richness	**Head** – guides your journey and how you make it	**Map your map** – so you understand all the choices you're free to make
		Change how you change – or you'll get what you always got
Thick trust – build long-term, sustainable relationships based on confidence, conviction and choice.	**Hand** – helps you work in partnership with others	**Step inside out** – and see the world the way others see it
		Share success – so it becomes sustainable: the only kind worth having

terms of how we think, feel and behave. As a result we can make decisions on a daily basis to manage how we lead ourselves. These decisions are just that – choices we have to make. Abstinence from such decisions leads to a leadership style that is weak, out of balance and generally ineffective for ourselves and others.

Your personal leadership style is constructed in the same way an architect might build a house (see Figure 4). The drivers are the foundations. If they're not rock-solid, the whole house will collapse.

The heart, head and hand dimensions form the structure of the building and define the overall shape, size and design limitations that the architect must operate within. They can be modified, but this takes time and will be constrained by the foundations. The decoration, style and overall appearance of the house involve decisions that can be made on a daily basis. So long as the drivers and dimensions are sound, all the necessary decisions can be made.

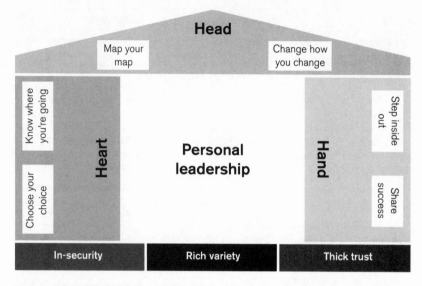

Figure 4 *Personal leadership construction*

The reason why so many leadership and effectiveness programs fail to deliver long-term sustainable improvement is that people are busy painting the window sills while, below, the foundations are collapsing.

If you wish to lead yourself and others more effectively, you have to deal with the drivers that dictate how you behave and look at the dimensions you already have in place. If you try to change your daily leadership choices without understanding the deeper aspects then you won't see long-term sustainable benefit.

Fortunately, the drivers and dimensions are not fixed. They can be changed. Don't kid yourself though. This book is no quick fix. Reshaping your life and leadership style is hard work. Substantial and sustainable personal change is difficult and painful. It's up to you.

But if the talent is lying dormant, the book will help release it. If you're prepared to make changes from your foundations up, you'll be amazed by the benefits and outcomes – they can be truly breathtaking.

heart
take control of your rudder

There are two kinds of people, those who finish what they start, and so on.

Robert Byrne

The heart dimension is the energy that drives us. It includes our emotions, beliefs, values and general sense of what we are here for and is the emotional nucleus of our personal leadership style. It's the belief system that helps us make vocational choices that affect the rest of our lives.

Get your hands off my rudder!

In simple terms, the heart is the guiding force that helps you make life choices. In his book *Emotional Intelligence*, Daniel Goleman talks about the inner rudder, the ability to make intuitive decisions based on subjective hunches or gut feelings. This rudder guides who we are, where we are heading and what course we can take.

Small twist – big turn
The plane rudder is a powerful thing because small changes in its direction effect awesome control over the craft. When it malfunctions, the consequences can be pretty disastrous. At height, it's possible for the pilot to correct errors and take back control of the plane, but lower down the consequences can be disastrous because the pilot doesn't have time to take remedial action.

Sometimes you can lose control of your inner rudder and suffer similar consequences. At best, the rudder might be slightly off center producing circular patterns in your life which means you end up going round in circles, never quite achieving what you set out to do. Decisions are made and seem to make sense in isolation but, because they lack a guiding sense or vision, you end up going back over previous journeys and never quite realizing your potential. You might believe you have control, but in reality any decision is being countermanded by the bow-wave effect of the previous decision.

In a worst case scenario, your inner rudder is unshackled, and flops from side to side. The result is that you're buffeted by external forces, losing the ability to make clear decisions. So you go through life constantly trying to get hold of new opportunities but always failing to really make any headway.

Like many people, I spent my early life being guided by the wishes of my parents. I even went into the same company as my father. Later, I succumbed to the drives of society, had a family and had a struggle to make ends meet. Only after I turned 38 did I really start to question what my driving goal was, what it is now, and most importantly, what it should be for the rest of my life.

I had to grab hold of the rudder while the boat was flailing around in a force eight gale with water leaking over the sides. But when you finally get control, it's a real pleasure.

Who controls your rudder?
Have you ever considered who really controls your rudder, to what extent you have control and in what way you've ceded control to others? Have they wrested it from your grasp, or have you given it up voluntarily? Consider the following questions:

◆ Who chooses when you go on holiday?

◆ Who chooses how you dress in the morning?

◆ Who chooses where and when you work?

◆ Who chooses how much you earn?

◆ Who chooses your next job?

- ◆ Who chooses your career direction?
- ◆ Who chooses who you are?

Can you really claim to have absolute control over all of these areas? If the answer is yes, then you do have a clear sense of choice and direction in your life. If, however, there are areas where you're not so sure, maybe you've given or traded away parts of your life to others. You probably made the exchange in return for a benefit, possibly a comfortable work life, high wages or a stake in the company. But, now you've traded partial control of your inner rudder to someone else, how happy are you? Is it a shared journey or do they tend to make all the key decisions? And can you regain control?

My concern is that as we go through life trading off parts of our inner rudder, we start to lose a sense of who we are.

The benevolent company might promise high wages, but the reality is that, with the dynamics of the new economy, such promises can be beyond their control. We are giving away our personal security to people and companies that might have no desire and capacity to guard it.

The net result is that rather than enhancing our personal security, we are potentially increasing our sense of insecurity, and our vulnerability.

Rudder ownership: from insecurity to *in*-security

Fame fades

So, where do you get your feel good factor and what happens when it disappears? Do you (or would you) perceive yourself to be a success in life because you earn a certain amount, have a BMW or live in a certain area? If so, what happens when that is taken away from you? Think about the people who marry film stars. Are they marrying that person for who they are or what they do? What happens when their fame fades?

The problem is that we measure each other and ourselves by what we have and do, rather than who we are. Think about the last time you went to a party and met someone new. The odds are that early on in the conversation one of your questions was 'what do you do for a living?' or 'where do you work?' This desire to label people and put them in a category based on what they do or how they earn a living is endemic in society and unfortunately conditioned from quite an early age. I remember at school how my friends used to compare their dads' wages and unofficial playground status would be accorded – my father being a cleaner didn't impress them much at all.

Look around and all you'll see is role confusion, as people fall into the trap of confusing who they are with what they do.

And we rely on these false badges of office. Look out for people on discussion or news programs. Someone is being interviewed and up flashes their name and job title. From this limited piece of information we are left to infer who this person is; their relevance to the discussion, their value to society and to themselves, and a whole host of other social badges that confer various degrees of status. For those lucky enough to have a flashy title or a grand badge, we can infer not only that they know what they're talking about, but that they know more than we do. Only when we get up close and take a personal view do we start to challenge this fictitious belief and remember that the badge is only a symbol of what they deliver in one unique situation. It's not an indication of who they really are.

Black holes of insecurity
The pull of these external security blankets that society provides is like the gravitational pull of a black hole. They have enormous energy, and the closer you get, the stronger the gravitational pull becomes, to a point where it's impossible to break away.

Try drawing a map of your life and consider the different black holes of insecurity you're attracted to (see Figure 5). These are the goals,

Figure 5 *Black holes of insecurity*

needs and desires that demand your time, energy and money – you believe you've 'made it' once you have them. Their upside is the personal satisfaction and buzz you get from having them; the downside is that, as with an addiction, you always have to have more.

I've seen it so many times with people who believe their goal in life is to get promoted. When you ask them why, they don't really know. It's just the gravitational pull from the you-must-have-a-powerful-job-title black hole that drives the need for importance. This drive for a corporate badge was highlighted in a survey of 1,500 workers where 70 per cent said they would rather have a fancier job title than a pay rise.[1] It's increasingly absurd, isn't it? If your company doesn't have a Paperclips Tzar, it probably has a Vice-President of Photocopying ...

In many ways, grand titles could bring more fun and creativity into organizations – like the Raging Inexorable Thunder Lizard Evangelist for a vice-president at the University of Texas Medical School – but few companies encourage this kind of creativity and, instead, titles are used as a substitute for the personal strength that comes from knowing who you are.

The real danger is when people believe that the power assigned to the title has been mystically transmuted to them and that they carry this power wherever they go.

In one organization I know, people were assigned operational codes that indicated their status. Each code consisted of up to three letters and three numbers in sequence. The make-up of the code meant that by simply looking to see how many characters were in the code, you could immediately determine the level of the individual within the corporate hierarchy. So if your designation was 'B', that would put you at director level, whereas AB1 might put you as a relatively senior manager, and ABC123 meant that you were the lowest of the low, generally a line manager. In meetings, people would introduce themselves, and they would immediately reel off their name and corporate code. To the uninitiated this might be seen as a minor issue, but it was a powerful tool for people to set the pecking order in a meeting. The *coup de grâce* would be the really senior manager who would hold back on his code until everyone else had said theirs before announcing his own with a grand flourish, like a wise old wizard pronouncing his status through the size of his wand.

In-security
Once you understand the principles contained in this book, no longer will the idea of insecurity be a negative and worrying concept. Instead, *in*-security, or inner-security, will mean what it says – that your personal security comes from within.

We need a form of leadership that draws on our ability to discard any notion of dependence on other people and objects.

Your own terror-free zone We've spent too much of our working lives scared – scared that we'll be laid off, yelled at, or blamed for something that wasn't our fault. And what have we learned? Fear doesn't motivate us for long. In the *Free-Agent Declaration of Independence*, Daniel H. Pink suggests that performers become great by playing in their own terror-free zone. We all have terror zones where demons reign, but we have the choice to face them head on, recognize them for what they are, and then exorcize them. The first step to shift from insecurity to *in*-security is to choose your choice.

OK, you're right, easier said than done. You could buy every word I say but the moment you walk into work tomorrow morning and meet the managing director of Global Enterprises, everything will go out the window. Insecurity comes from years and years of social conditioning that is rarely unlocked with the wave of a wand. But it can be controlled and used as the energy to drive your inner security, with the aid of three things, from you, yourself:

◆ the passion to make difficult choices and describe where and when each stage of the journey will be complete

◆ clarity of thought to understand what maps you must use to manage your journey

◆ the ability to work with others and, in doing so, achieve shared success.

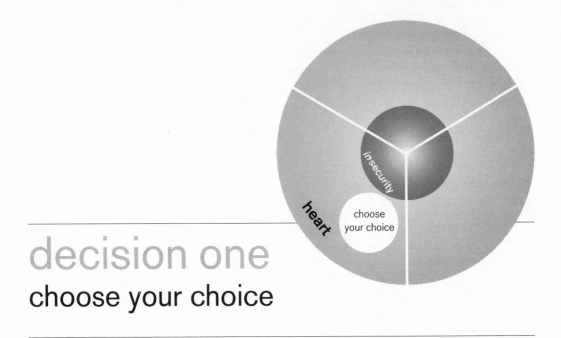

decision one
choose your choice

Destiny is not a matter of chance, it is a matter of choice, it is not a thing
to be waited for, it is a thing to be achieved.

William Jenning Bryan

So what's the big deal? you ask. I make choices all the time. Yes, of course you do, but are they the optimum choices?

Within the choose your choice decision there are five ideas to consider:

- ◆ **Micro-choice** – the extent to which you are able to manage choice on a second by second basis and stop doing the things that you look back on with anger or regret.

- ◆ **Choice muscle** – how choice is like a muscle, the more you use it the stronger it gets.

- ◆ **Corporate slavery** – just sit back and consider the extent to which your work 'for' or 'with' your company.

- ◆ **Choice pendulum** – total choice give you total freedom, but within such a position you can be seen as selfish. The essence is to balance your choice with the needs of others to reach a position where you share success.

- ◆ **Greasy pole** – once we have the power to make choices we must ensure that they are focused on areas where we can effect a change and not on issues that are not within our power to resolve.

Unless you have the power to take choices and the wisdom to make the right ones then the notion of personal leadership is a vague dream that many aspire to but less achieve.

Micro-choice

Often we abstain from facing real decisions, instead leaving it to fate – effectively choosing not to choose. Choice abstinence takes place in all three dimensions – heart, head and hand.

Heart: lost in the red mist

What happens when you're driving along and someone pulls out in front of you. Get frustrated or angry? Most of the time we're able to contain these emotions but there are occasions when we let our emotions take over (remember shouting at the neighbours because of their loud music, or when you got really peeved at the shop assistant because they weren't quite sure how to use the new till?) and the red mist of anger leads us to take revenge on the perceived 'imbecile'. But the joy of retribution is often overtaken by the cold dawn of reality. It probably wasn't all their fault and, even if it was, the pain felt by the recipient of your outburst isn't going to help develop any future relationship.

Could we really have restrained our anger and controlled our feelings for that split second? It might be difficult, but difficult isn't the same as impossible.

People can and do develop strategies to ensure that their emotions don't become harmful forces that take over their lives.

Head: I just can't make it

We also make head non-choices in the way we think things through – very often when we're faced with a problem our standard solutions can't resolve. I sometimes see this with my children when they have a homework problem. The schooling process often constrains them to process ideas and thoughts in a linear way. The moment they face a problem that is slightly outside their comfort zone they believe they don't know the answer and therefore can't solve it. Like someone stuck on an underground train that has broken down, they just sit and wait for someone else to come along and repair the fault and take them on their journey. When I give my kids 'the answer', I fix their problem short-term but create a bigger long-term predicament. By doing that, I reinforce their belief that there's only one solution and that it's pointless to look for any other way to solve the issue, as well as reinforcing their intellectual dependency. But by challenging them to think around the problem, they can learn to recognize that they have other choices and ways to resolve difficulties.

Hand: OK, just one more drink!
Finally, we can take hand non-choices in the way we behave. Think about the last time you got blinding drunk at the office party; you woke up the next morning with the obligatory hangover and memory loss, you choose to blame the drink, the people who invited you, or the fact that it was the last Friday in the month and your pay-cheque had just arrived. The reality is that we *choose* to behave in such a way. At the point where the choice must be made (to have the Virgin Mary or Bloody Mary), we abstain from any sense of reality and choose not to take the better option.

In all of these examples, I have tried to look at instances where we may think, feel or behave in a way that seems 'normal'. However, normal isn't always good for us. We have the capacity to choose our choice, even when that choice seems uncomfortable, risky or confrontational. The test must always be: 'Am I making this choice based on what other people want, or am I responding in a way that fits with my personal values and beliefs?'

Don't shout: just shun
Choose your choice is less about the freedom to choose actions, plans and journeys, it's more about taking control of your inner thoughts and feelings. In the first instance, it's about giving yourself the power and freedom to choose your response to a given situation. You can choose how to respond to an irate customer, a crying child or an irritating relative who has just turned up on your doorstep. You can choose to behave in a negative way, but you do have the capacity to choose your choices and respond in a better, more appropriate way. The acid test of a good choice is often: 'Will I look back in anger or regret at this decision?'

The Amish have the custom of ignoring or not responding to those who break their social code. They shun them and turn them into non-persons. Bear them in mind next time you receive poor service. You don't need to get upset or rant. You have the choice to simply say no, and choose not to go back to that place again. And don't imagine that avoiding confrontation has no consequence. The reality is that if they continue to offer the same poor service, the business will eventually fail. So, you don't need to get upset at people who upset you. You can just feel really good in the knowledge that you have erased them from your personal map. The message is don't shout – just shun.

And developing the ability to make internal choices about how you feel, think and behave isn't going to turn you into a sterile robot creature who feels nothing. There's no need to spend hours carefully analyzing each problem. It will free your emotions up to think, feel or act in a way that will help you lead yourself and others in a far more effective way. Believe me, it's not just liberating, it's a lot less stressful.

Just choose not to bitch about your boss behind their back when they don't give you a good monthly review; choose not to get irate when there's a tricky problem to be solved; choose to say sorry to your boss or team member when you make a mistake.

Push the pause button
I used to work for someone who had a real problem. He would turn up every day at around 9.30am, spend an hour in the office talking with his friends and then head off down the bar. When he got back around 2pm he was well and truly over the driving limit. My problem was that if I couldn't get a morning slot in his diary I would end up with the afternoon slot. When this happened I would be frustrated because he was drunk and I wouldn't be able to get the message across to him. My response to my own frustration was either fight or flight. I would walk through the door ready to go into battle, or I would just send an e-mail instead. Even when I got a morning slot, I was so uptight about the previous afternoon's session that I would always have a poor meeting. The red mist in front of my

eyes ultimately led to me taking the first alternative job that I could find.

It dawned on me later that the failure was actually mine. I was being paid to deliver a product and clearly I let this person influence and reduce my capability to do this. I failed to choose my choice because I had failed to choose my response. I should have pushed the pause button and stopped to think about what I wanted to get out of the relationship; how I was reacting to his style; how I should be responding in order to achieve the goals I'd set for myself.

A key principle of the heart dimension is that we have to choose our response to others' actions. I should have taken responsibility for my own behaviour – my own actions. On reflection I could have managed it in many different ways – but I let my responses be dictated by the other person's actions. As a result, my ability to operate effectively was reduced and I allowed someone else's behaviour to dictate my career path.

Consider times you look back and think 'if only' – 'if only I hadn't behaved that way or made that comment, it might be different now'. Just take an hour or so to look back at all the times you reacted or over-reacted to another person's emotions, ideas or behaviours. Try to think how else you might have behaved and what the consequences of that action might have been.

Clearly you can't choose the consequences of any actions you take, but you must be prepared to live with them, as they are a result of your behaviour.

Not accepting the consequences means that you're trying to absolve yourself from both sides of the equation, and that's not possible.

Think about a relationship you have which is less than effective. Ask yourself: 'What do they do that I react to?' Try to think of a positive way you could react to their behaviour. Plan to deliver this behaviour the next time you meet them. If it doesn't work the first time, keep trying until it becomes a habit so you no longer respond to the things that trigger your irritation.

Choice muscle

As you start to flex your ability to make choices, a powerful transformation will occur. Just like the growing strength of a muscle, the ability to make small choices leads to an enhanced capacity for bigger and bigger choices. So, as you enhance your desire and ability to lead yourself, this in turn enhances your ability to lead others. People will sense that you have a level of strength and discipline in your life and will look to you for support and guidance.

Just think about the people you turn to for advice and assistance. You probably picked them because you recognized intuitively that they have the ability to make choices when facing difficult circumstances. The more you choose to choose, the more, in turn, you'll be asked to help with the choices others have to make. The possibilities are endless. You'll make contact with more and more people who have the capacity to choose their choice and you'll help people transform their lives. The world you'll be operating in will be characterized by freedom, challenge and alternatives.

We can choose to choose
The only choice they give you is one you gave them in the first place. So don't be thankful when your company says it's going to allow you more space to make decisions or that they are going to run an empowerment programme. This is a capability you already have, and your taking up their 'offer' is just an indication of how much personal choice and control you have traded away.

Other people don't give you the power of choice.

Choice is lost over time though gradual erosion (see Figure 6). In childhood, we have the absolute beliefs that we have the freedom to

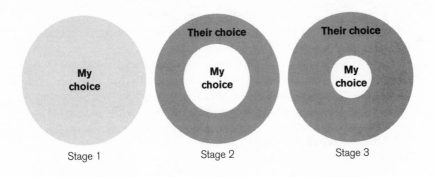

Stage 1 Stage 2 Stage 3

Figure 6 *Choice erosion*

make decisions we believe are right. As a child we want what we want, and we want it now and we'll scream the supermarket down if we don't get it.

Erosion starts when we have to adhere to the constraints and disciplines of other people, for example, parents and teachers looking for the most painless ways to manage their lives. As we start school and work we have to trade in our right to choose in order to ensure some level of success. Then, at some point, the choices we have traded away exceed the freedoms we are left with. The net result is that we are in the choice trap. We have given away our freedom to make choices and the only way to recover it is to give up the trappings of success we'd so eagerly pursued.

The way to stretch our choice muscle is to draw a personal leadership boundary. Part of this decision will involve a risk and reward trade-off. But you can't have your cake and eat it.

If your company has paid to take over your right of choice in certain areas, you must return something in order to regain control of those aspects that are important to you.

A question of balance
The first step is easy – draw two circles. In the inner circle, write those aspects of your life where you want to choose your choice, and

in the outer one put those aspects that you're happy to trade. Once complete you should end up with a picture like the one in Figure 7.

The idea is for you to take back the things that choice erosion has taken over during your lifetime. Don't worry, you don't have to give your car to charity to rid yourself of material slavery. But before you can start to lead yourself, you do have to recognize the extent to which you have given away your freedom of choice. If you're happy in a situation where the outer circle overlaps with your inner circle because it offers you the financial freedom and comfort you desire, then fine. But you'll need to understand the balance between the two and the risks that go with your level of choice. You have the right to choose the boundaries of your choice area; the important thing is to take time to understand just what the boundaries are and how you can influence them.

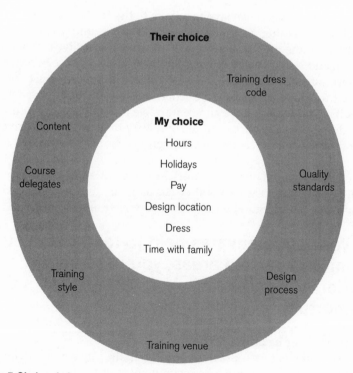

Figure 7 *Choice circle*

Corporate slavery

Corporations are great financial providers but they don't often enable people to realize their true (and hidden) potential. I frequently meet people who just switch off their heart when they get to work. David Mamet suggests that we permit ourselves to be treated like commodities in the hope that we may one day be regarded as valuable commodities. It's this subordination to others' wishes that offers short-term gain but leads to long-term regret over failed personal potential.

Do you say I work 'for' or 'with'?
Quick test – if someone asks what you do for a living, do you respond with 'I work for ... ' or 'I work with ... '? The importance of this statement can never be underestimated. By simple use of the phrase 'I work for ... ' you're indicating a sense of personal slavery in exchange for a living wage. Such a mindset helps neither the individual nor the company. For the individual, it's disempowering. For the organization, it results in disempowered, disinterested employees, determined to end the day as soon as possible so they can go home and do the things they really want to do. Vast amounts of money are spent on empowerment, motivational and inspirational programs, but it's a bit like the alcoholic who goes out every morning to buy a bottle of Scotch and then spends all afternoon in counselling. The support in the afternoon is all well and good, but the focus should be on not buying the drink in the first place. So when an organization spends their money on such personal development programs, they're fighting a losing battle.

But there is a way to change this. Rather than saying you work 'for' someone, think, feel and behave in a way that suggests you work 'with' them as an emotional, if not trading, partner. Become a business within a business. This is the challenge for people who, in contrast to operating in an open market, operate in a political market – working for someone else in a medium/large company.

A new way to feel, think and behave: from Type 1 to Type 2
In order to take this step we need to rethink the underlying economic model applied in most businesses. When a company recruits an employee, it generally does so on the economic model shown in Figure 8. The employee is assumed to be owned by the company and gives up the risk associated with operating in a competitive and open market, in turn relinquishing much of the margin on their personal capital.

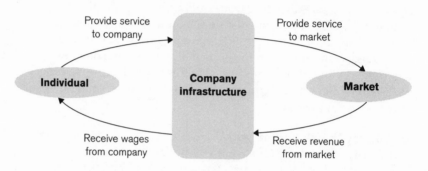

Figure 8 *Type 1 thinking*

This economic model made sense a world when the ability to create a market relied on the ownership of land, labor and capital, but does it make sense in a world where revenue is driven by customer access and the ideas that people like? If you have personal capital that is valued by the market, why should you give such a large piece of yourself away and act as a corporate slave? You exchange income for the security of a large company and all the associated benefits.

But this model is twenty years out of date and, with the shift to a knowledge economy, the whole notion of large-company security is nonsense. There is no more long-term security in a large company – so why give such a large chunk of your personal capital to them?

Time for a new way of thinking, Type 2 thinking, as illustrated in Figure 9. Time to take responsibility for your personal capital. Start to lead yourself and lead others in a totally new way. In Type 2

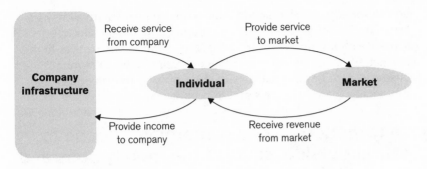

Receive service
from company

Provide service
to market

Company
infrastructure

Individual

Market

Provide income
to company

Receive revenue
from market

Figure 9 *Type 2 thinking*

thinking, choices and decisions are based on the fact that you, the individual, generate virtual or real revenue from the market and choose to give a percentage of your income to the company infrastructure as a reward for them giving you access to the market.

By looking at your relationships from this perspective, you can start to understand the supply and demand profiles in more depth. No longer are you cushioned from the realities of life by the corporate machine. Instead you view yourself as 'Me Inc.', with all the problems of brand development, market entry and financial control.

With the Type 2 model, I am not advocating that we all give up our corporate careers and become sole traders. What I'm saying is that everyone within a company, from the receptionist to the managing director, should look at their role as market provider. What is your true commercial value to the business? Who are your primary customers? How do you measure personal success? And most important of all, what is your value on the open market? In this way we all become more conscious of the value of our own personal capital and start to make real choices as to where this value is best placed in order to realize the best market return.

'So what?' (as my editor, Rachael, said). The theory's fine but what does this mean on a Monday morning when it's raining, the boss is grouchy and the in-tray is overflowing. The funny thing is that this is when the difference is most important, and most apparent. Imagine walking in to work on a Monday morning and seeing the overflowing in-tray and the moody boss. You react in a negative way, and the down-cycle begins. You look fed up, the boss has a pop, you respond with an attack; further comments fly across the room and you're already branded as someone who can't cope with a busy in-tray. This is a symptom of Type 1 thinking, where you work 'for' someone else. With Type 2 thinking, the in-tray is your access to the market. It's the way that your revenue stream flows into your business. A full in-tray means 'market opportunity'; an empty in-tray means 'panic, no one's making contact'.

So, if you go in to work on Monday morning, choose to ignore the weather outside, smile at the moody boss and attack the in-tray with hunger, the chances are that your internal brand value will increase and lead to improved work opportunities.

Type 2 thinking is demanding and certainly isn't easy for people who have been conditioned into Type 1 thinking. However, the rewards are worth the effort.

Choice pendulum

Too little of the heart, head or hand dimensions results in under performance, but too much can result in a lop-sided or prejudiced leadership style. Think of choice as a pendulum – any degree of misalignment puts the swing out of kilter and the clock out of time. A pendulum retains its stability because it moves from left to right with a swing that is constant in travel and timing and centers around a balanced center point.

Personal leadership framework is built on the idea of balance and alignment.

When we abstain, consciously or subconsciously, or trade options on our lives, we can end up corporate slaves. The pendulum is pulled over to the far right-hand side (see Figure 10). In this position, you have little real choice in your life and it's difficult to pull back to a position of control.

If you allow the pendulum to swing in the other direction, it's just as unstable and likely to topple over (see Figure 11). The danger is that

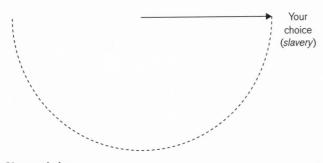

Your
choice
(*slavery*)

Figure 10 *Slavery choice*

Figure 11 *Selfish choice*

the choose-your-choice message can be taken too literally. Imagine the person who's totally wrapped up in their ability to control and manage every single aspect of their life. They might be a real kingpin in terms of life management but you'd avoid them like the plague. An over-zealous approach to the choose-your-choice dimension can result in you being seen as selfish and egotistical.

A sense of balance needs to be achieved by taking a mid-way position (see Figure 12). You take a stance based on a collaborative and interactive approach that allows you to make your personal choices in the spirit of sharing. As a spouse or partner, parent, manager or coach, for example, you make your own choices where the others in the relationship are concerned, but when formulating your decision, it's made on the basis of a shared set of values and principles.

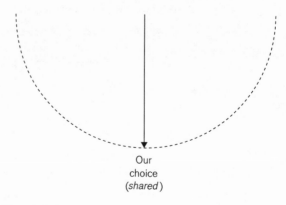

Figure 12 *Shared choice*

All long-term effective relationships are grounded in the position where all the parties have attained the power to choose their choice. By shifting to a shared-choice position the individuals are not giving up any power within their personal leadership. Much of the driving force for a balanced, centered position stems from the *in*-security driver. If someone is driven by their personal insecurity, they will be loath to share choice because it feels as though they are losing power over their lives. Where the *in*-security driver drives someone, they are happy to share choice and power because they are comfortable that all their personal power comes from within.

When both parties lose the power to choose their choice and in effect give control to the other person, it places the relationship in a weak position. It leads to a spirit of second-guessing, double-checking, unspoken arguments and undiscussable feelings. If you see evidence of this type of behaviour in any relationship, look for signs of choice imbalance. Someone is not managing their right and freedom to make choices.

Think about the people you work or live with. Imagine where you would place each of them on the choice pendulum. Do they operate from a selfish basis and make decisions based on their needs only? Do they always watch their choice of TV channel? Buy the food they like? Or do they always make decisions influenced by what you want? Maybe there's someone who works for you and all they ever do is agree with you? Perhaps you choose to work or live with these people because you're locked into a relationship or because they satisfy a particular need in you. But the question to ask yourself is: To what extent are you really taking control of the situation and leading yourself and them? Would the relationship be even more effective if you were able to share choices? Could you agree what things are important for you and for the others in the relationship and then make more choices based on this shared understanding?

Climb down the greasy pole

I see many people avoid the pain of choice by building personal avoidance strategies. They enact ways to legitimately avoid making decisions. We've all been in meetings where a tough decision had to be made. But rather than dealing with the issue, you stray off into 'isn't it awful ... ' or 'it's their fault' territory rather than dealing with the real problem. Think about the last argument with your partner – that you didn't have. You know those awful periods when you have a gripe with each other, but have both decided not to talk about it for fear of unearthing some real issues that will be difficult to confront and resolve. You end up bickering about the washing up instead.

I have seen entire organizations behave this way. Companies consistently talk and act on all of the silly things that irritate the business, and ignore the fact that their market is slipping away and they'll soon be in a 'fix or die' position.

Don't let the crap turn into crisis
While our emotions are caught up in a maelstrom of defensive anger and frustration over something trivial and pointless, the real issues are being ignored.

The trick to successful personal leadership is to point the emotional energy and focus into an area where it can deliver a tangible solution. One that will resolve the root problem, not the symptoms.

Look at any company going through a difficult time and ask the people where the emotional energy within the company is being focused. What does the chairman talk about every day? And what is the time and money being spent on? I guarantee that in most cases the emotional energy is being spent on those things that can't be resolved by the managers: the new tax rate, the overseas competition or the currency exchange rate. Certain circumstances and conditions might well cause problems, but the questions to be asked must always be: Can you change them? And do you have control over these issues right now? If not, try and convince the people who *can* change them, or move on to things that *you* can change.

This displacement of energy is (here's a new technical term for you) greasy pole syndrome (Figure 13). Anyone who has managed to get to the top of a greasy pole expends all their energy trying to stop

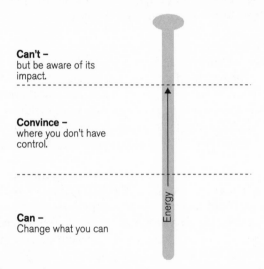

Can't –
but be aware of its
impact.

Convince –
where you don't have
control.

Can –
Change what you can

Energy

Figure 13 *Greasy pole*

themselves sliding down. It might be fun sitting up there, but the energy expenditure doesn't really do anything useful. It's constantly focused on things that can't change. But it's far more productive to come down to the bottom of the pole and focus some emotion and energy on things that can be changed. And only use your energy on things beyond your control if you're influencing the influencers.

Expend energy convincing those people who can deliver change. Otherwise, don't waste it – it's too valuable.

Let me put this in context. After five years at the top of my greasy pole in one corporation I worked for, redundancies were announced and I (along with many other people) panicked. I started to spend all my time worrying about what would happen if I were the one to go, about how life might be, and harking back to the good old days. I spent my time wishing for a white knight to come along and save the company. I spent my time reading the internal job news looking for safe bolt-holes where I could hide away until the storm had passed. I didn't expend energy on improved performance so I would be the one to stay. I didn't manage my network so that I could help people understand the value I added. I didn't pull my finger out and get new experience and qualifications. In essence, all my emotional energy was spent at the top of my greasy pole, looking really busy and energetic, but in reality doing little to enhance my personal position. Don't make the same mistakes I made.

You can hit the target
We have a choice in how we allocate our emotions and energy. Next time you're in a meeting and people start to lament the failure of the senior managers or 'them up there', choose not to go there, focus on the real issues instead. Challenge the group to map what is in their power to resolve, and what factors are beyond their control. Then work on what you can do.

The beauty is that as the group becomes more practised at operating in the 'can' and 'convince' areas (see Figure 14) it will automatically self-correct and fix itself when the vague 'can't' issues surface. The net result is that the emotions of the group will be energized, there will be improved decision-making capability, and deliverable actions will be agreed, not pie-in-the-sky solutions. As a group you'll make the decision to choose your choice.

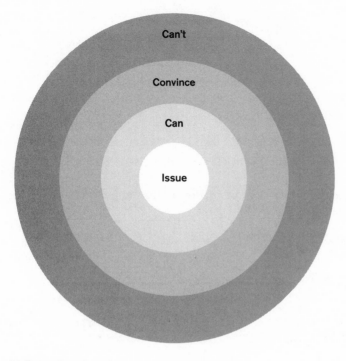

Figure 14 *Greasy target*

Choose your choice: quick summary

The decision to choose your choice is grounded in the following ideas:

◆ Other people can't give you freedom of choice. You start life with a full box of choices and as you grow older you may choose to barter them away in exchange for other benefits. Other people only exercise control over your choices because you allow them to.

◆ The life you have today is a product of the choices you have made. The life you want tomorrow will be achieved with the choices you make today. Choose your next choice carefully.

◆ By choosing your choice you increase your personal power. Ultimately you will influence the people who have influence over you.

◆ You own and are responsible for the impact of your choices, and their consequences.

◆ Sometimes choice is about not taking action or responding to the way that others behave towards you. It's harder to say 'I won't' than it is to say 'I will'.

◆ Choice isn't always about what you want to do; you can choose to create a shared success with other partners.

◆ Your most important choices involve disregarding the things you can't change and concentrating on the things you can.

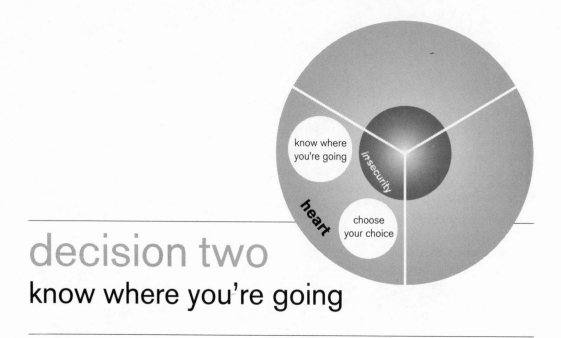

decision two
know where you're going

You don't understand I could have had class.
I could have been a contender.
I could have been somebody.
Instead of a bum, which is what I am – let's face it.

Marlon Brando, in *On the Waterfront*

Personal leadership is founded in the notion that we should have a clear and defined outcome for any journey, that is, know where we're going. This clarity will offer a clear and purposeful vision to ourselves and others. I am not suggesting that everything we do in life should be rigidly controlled with a finite and planned outcome, just that we should aspire to know what we want to achieve and why. In developing a clear goal for our personal or business life we can take away the pain of indecision, overcome insecurity, and avoid the confusion that arises when we are pulled in different directions.

Although you might believe that you know where you're going, there is often a deeper internal tension that pulls you in many directions.

Think about the last time you had to make an important decision. Did you feel any unease about making the choice? If you did, then the different parts of you were trying to make the decision in competition with each other.

We lead three lives, each driven by the three dimensions of heart, head and hand. The hand is the part of us that others see. The head view is how we think, the rational. The heart is how we feel, or the third, secret inner life that only we know. When aligned, we have a clear sense of purpose. We can make a decision almost without thinking because the dimensions are working together. But when the heart, head and hand journeys are separated it leads to internal tension and frustration, and in turn anxiety or guilt.

Imagine you've just won the lottery. How will you spend the money? The heart says take those flying lessons you've dreamed of since you were a child. The head suggests stocks and shares. The hand choice might be to do what your friends suggest and have a party, just blow it all on the biggest gig in town. This indecision and dilemma might last for a second or it might last for a year. However long, such internal debate can lead to anxiety and tension both internally and in all your relationships. (PS: Opt for the party!)

heart

lead yourself

momentum

Where you have clear personal purpose, such indecision will be minimized. You'll know where you're going, have a clear outcome and be able to describe to others what's important now and in the future. Once you have such a clear and unambiguous view of your journey and the heart, hand and head choice come together in a single, unified idea, then any choice will be really easy to make. But only by having a clear sense of where you're heading can you be sure that decisions you make today will be of value tomorrow.

Within the know-where-you're-going choice, there are six factors to consider:

- ◆ **Distraction disease.** All our journeys start with good intent, but along the way we get sidelined by gifts and goodies, like job titles and thoughts of status, that erode who we are.

- ◆ **Choice mapping.** Step back and forward in time to understand the balance between the choices you make and the choices you give to others.

- ◆ **Bingo ball behaviour.** Often people are allowed to play too great a role in influencing who you are and where you're going.

- ◆ **Chunk up.** Never plan your future from your current view point. Always climb the mast to get a view of the horizon and see your options with a broader perspective.

- ◆ **Turn on the potential tap.** When planning where you're going, make sure you draw on your full potential.

- ◆ **OUTCOME testing.** Make sure that when you define where you're going you have both the will and capability to get there. Avoid at all costs the new year's resolution where you set your goal in a flurry of excitement and motivation, only to realize how impossible the goal is a few days later.

Distraction disease

External distractions can knock us off course and make other things seem more attractive than the journey we initially embarked on. These distractions can be power, money, titles or the latest household gadget that you simply must have.

I didn't appreciate the distraction of title-ism until I nearly got knocked out.

I had made the big step from being a sales support officer to sales manager. The sheer shock, excitement and power that the title gave me was quite staggering. All of a sudden I had the ability to say what was right, decide the fate of people who were 'below' me, and power, oh, power, lead the performance review, when I could sit back and tell people just how much they had upset me all year long.

Then along came the Christmas party, the ideal chance to strut my stuff and display the power badge – a 'new suit'. All was fine until the end of the night. There was a guy who was as big as an ox and probably about five times as strong. He'd hit the cocktail bowl big time and was getting out of order. After a while he became really agitated and wanted to thump someone. So I put on my managerial hat, strolled up to him and, in my most commanding, managerial voice, ordered him to grow up and go home. Feeling pretty proud of myself and having asserted my managerial status to the group, I saw his right fist speeding towards me. At that point, I had a revelation: just because I think I'm a manager it doesn't mean that anyone else does! Luckily, my black eye faded, but the lesson has stuck with me to this day!

heart

lead yourself

momentum

If you're trying to calm someone who is drunk and highly agitated, you're dependent on personal power to influence how they see the world through the red mist of alcohol. The whole problem was that I confused who I was with what I did. The figure of Mick Cope The Manager had temporarily obscured the view of Mick Cope The Individual.

Robin Seymour and John Cleese have explored this idea in an excellent book called *Life and How to Survive It*. They consider the notion that people place the role of work over personal life for a number of reasons. First of all, it gives people a relatively easy way of deriving a sense of purpose rather than having to look at the more personal areas of their lives like relationships with loved ones. It's far easier to concentrate on the quarterly sales figures or performance targets than to sit down with your partner and openly discuss what you mean to each other, what you believe in and where you want to go in the coming years. Seymour and Cleese also suggest that it helps to structure our time. Rather than having to sit and think, we anxiously rush around looking busy and in the process help ourselves feel important. The down side is that one day the panic stops, we retire or have to slow down, and people can't cope with the freedom, space and time they are offered. It's only when these emotional blinkers are torn off that we realize we've wasted a lot of our life up to that point. The danger is that we let work become more important than life and end up playing a well known corporate game called 'Whoever has the most toys when they die wins'.[2]

The loss of me
The worrying thing is that this erosion of who I am through the acquisition of what I do is introduced at such an early age. Take a few minutes to think about when the shift started for you and the route you've taken. What you come up with might be surprisingly similar to mine.

It really scares me to look at this list (it was even scarier to write it) because it highlights just how much I've been sucked in by other people's insecurity magnets. Even worse is the fact the insecurity pulls seem to grow in strength and number as I get older, and the end result is it becomes even harder to break away from their gravity and take control of my life.

Child	Teenager	Adult	Parent
Drive to acquire toys that are in fashion	Need baggy pants to look cool	Must renew the car every two years	Must have the right pushchair for the children
Pressure from teacher to climb the league table	Must have flowery shirts made by Brutus	Social conditioning to buy house in the right area	Must be able to buy the children the correct computer games
Must have Johnny Seven machine gun (as seen on TV)	Must have alloy wheels on the car (even though they cost more than the car)	Oh no, I don't have a degree: I'm not as good as my manager	Need to ensure that children's friends don't see me driving around in my old Toyota van
	Must have the right haircut	Oh no, I'm getting fat: start the diet treadmill	Must have the correct brand label clothes for the teenage children
	Must have Ben Sherman shirt	Oh my god, the gardening show says we must have decking: quick, buy it and DIY it before the next barbecue	

From an early age we start to trade creativity for compliance, school rules, exam marks, then company games.

Dare to deviate from the norm and you risk losing a bonus or promotion. All the time this is happening, there's a gradual erosion of your personal security and self-reliance, as you replace who you are for what you do.

The end result is often an *in*-security ramp, indicating the gradual shift during our lives that takes the focus from who we are to what we do (see Figure 15). So, over time, we are allowed (and allow ourselves) to spend less time and energy on the inner-self, and instead place greater emphasis on the acquisition of external badges and artefacts. Although we might see a short-term reward in this strategy, we risk giving away control of our lives to other people and things.

True personal leadership must come from the inner strength of who I am rather than what I do. As you go through life you experience a

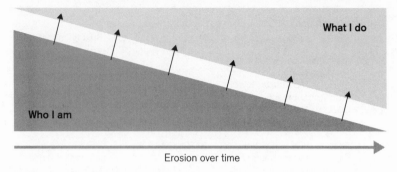

What I do

Who I am

Erosion over time

Figure 15 *Insecurity ramp*

range of roles, work functions and responsibilities. If you changed your personal leadership style every time you moved to a new position you would be like a bingo ball bouncing around yet always under the control of the caller. It's far better to know who we are deep down and use this as the launch pad to drive what we do more effectively.

Knowing where you're going doesn't require a huge project plan or an electronic organizer full of 'to do's'. It's just a clear and succinct idea that indicates who you are and where you're going.

Think of Martin Luther King's famous address. Even in a single sentence he manages to capture the essence of his beliefs, values and dreams – all who listen to or read the address are clear as to his direction:

I have a dream that my four children will one day live in a nation where they will not be judged by the color of their skin but by the content of their character.

I have a dream today.

How would you describe your dreams, beliefs, passion and future goals?

◆ What are your core values?

◆ What are your partner's and family's values?

◆ What do you want to be doing in one , three and five years' time?

◆ What personal dreams impact the future of your family, friends and work colleagues?

◆ What will you say 'no' to?

◆ What are the three things that guide all your important decisions?

Do you have a clear definite response? Test if you truly have a clear outcome by asking your friends, family and peers to answer the same questions about you. If they can give the same answers you gave, then you do know where you're going. If not, then try to define the gap.

heart

lead yourself

momentum

Choice mapping

On the basis that we live in a borrowed body that has to be returned, just think about what you've done with your life so far. List all the things that you've achieved and try to reflect on the extent to which they occurred through happenstance or coincidence. Try to remember whether you chose them or whether they were at the behest (partial or fully) of someone else? On reflection, are they things you're pleased to have achieved or would you prefer to have done something else?

Now think about what you are going to do in your life. List the great things you'll deliver, the holidays and the special moments with your grandchildren. Is the second question harder? If so, is this because you trust someone else to decide what you'll do? Is it because you don't believe that the future can be predicted? Or is it because life has been fine without any planning, so why change now?

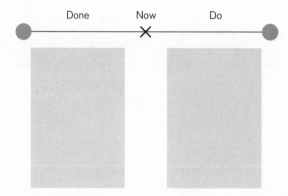

Figure 16 *Past and projected maps*

Now take the past and projected list shown in Figure 16 and break it into four components: the choices you have taken and those others have taken for you; and the choices you plan to take and those you plan to let others take for you. You should end up with something like the Choice map in Figure 17.

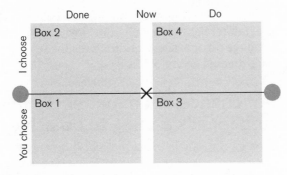

Figure 17 *Choice timeline*

As you map out the choices you've made and the choices that you wish to make, be realistic about which ones you place in each of the boxes.

◆ **Box 1.** On reflection, if someone else made the choice for you, might you have been able to make it yourself or were you in a position where any alternative would have been impossible. If so, how could you have pre-managed the situation to avoid being in that position?

◆ **Box 2.** For these choices, are you really convinced you had absolute control over the choice? Are you sure that no one else had a partial role in driving or influencing your choice?

◆ **Box 3.** If you predict that others will have a role to play in making your future choices, how comfortable are you with this? Would you like to change the situation and move the choice to Box 4? And what action can you take now to wrest control back from the other people or organizations. If you do this, what impact will it have on your relationships with them? What are the risks associated with such action and what personal liabilities do you have that will be a barrier to such action?

◆ **Box 4.** What do you need to have in place to ensure that these choices stay your own and are not gently pulled into Box 3 over time? Do you have the necessary financial, moral, political and/or relational freedom to take such a degree of control over your life, or will debts rear their head to stop you from making real personal decisions?

I don't believe in the power of prediction but I do believe in the power of choice. I don't believe that all your dreams will come true – but if you don't have dreams and work towards them, all you'll get is someone else's dreams given to you.

Destiny isn't a matter of chance, it's a matter of choice; it isn't a thing to be waited for, it's a thing to be achieved.

When you indicate what you'll do, this isn't meant to be a firm projection of what will happen but it's the place where you set out the stall for the future so that you, your family, your peers and your colleagues all have a clear understanding of what is important for you and where you're going.

Bingo ball behavior

Think about the last time you were lost on a trip. It might be the overseas holiday when you ventured down a strange street and started to worry for the safety of your family. It might even be the first day of a new job when you started to worry how on earth you would find your way to the toilets. Familiar to each case is a sense of anxiety, confusion and fear of the unknown. You're in a place where there are no directions, guides or help of any kind. Now remember the feeling when you found the first landmark that you recognized. It might be a familiar junction on the freeway, the sound of a church bell or the board room. Whatever the landmark, it's something that gives you a stake in the ground and a basis on which to make a decision. It's this sense of orientation and location that is so important within the personal leadership framework. The ability to find a reference point in times of turmoil and confusion is an essential part of any leadership process.

My life as a bingo ball

Think of someone you know who goes through life without any real sense of purpose or direction. It might be that fate is always on hand to offer a guiding hand or help, but for most of us, this isn't the case.

People without purpose have no boundaries (see Figure 18), no understanding of what is good or bad advice, with the result that they respond (and believe) different advice on differing days like a bouncing ball in a bingo machine.

Consider the life of Billy, a trainee manager at a large computing company. He is about to attend a promotion interview that could really make a big difference to his income. At the start of the week he has a clear plan to spend his time preparing for next week's interview. However, after a couple of hours person A comes along and suggests that preparation is of little use because the job is sewn up and will go to someone else. So Billy decides that it's not worth spending time and goes off to do some other work. He then meets B over coffee and she says that the job isn't sewn up at all, they are just looking for someone with a special set of skills. So Billy rushes to the resource centre to track down some reports. At the resource centre, Billy meets an old friend who is also going to be interviewed. They suggest that the team manager is biased against people with long hair, so Billy rushes out to get a haircut. These diversions continue right up to the interview, and Billy will fail to get the job.

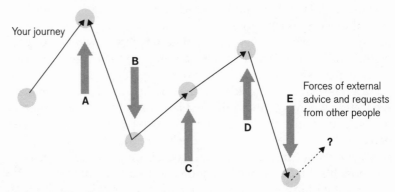

Your journey

B

A

Forces of external advice and requests from other people

E

D

C

?

Figure 18 *Open boundaries*

So there we have Bingo Ball Billy, someone who responds to forces from all directions because he doesn't really know where he's going. The alternative is to build a picture that sets out where you're heading and to follow that journey. By setting out the parameters of your journey you can define a corridor or window of opportunity which consists of those things you are prepared to do; everything else falls outside the boundary (see Figure 19). For Bingo Ball Billy's next interview, he would need to define who he will listen to, what subjects he will study, who he won't listen to, and what topic areas he will not research. He might go so far as to define what he wants from the job and under what circumstances he will reject any offer.

Your life doesn't have to become unchangeable and set in concrete. As your life circumstances change, you respond and adapt accordingly. But when this happens it's easier to change the

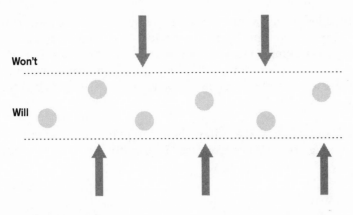

Figure 19 *Decision corridor*

operating boundary and be guided by a clear set of principles, rather than trying to make each decision in isolation.

An early one for me was the decision not to move house. The company I worked for at the time was in reorganization frenzy – every other month there would be a reorganization and accompanying relocation. I looked around and saw my colleagues' lives being turned upside down and in some cases relationships destroyed as they responded to choices made by the company. My choice was not to move my family, but to include the flexibility to travel further to work. So, if push came to shove (and it did) I would lodge out for a period to maintain my career but not put my partner and children through the upheaval of moving house and school. Having made this choice, it became very easy to make a career decision. There was no turmoil or tension if promotion came along in an area where I could not commute. It was simply outside the corridor and therefore not an option.

Enter the choice corridor
Once you've defined your choice corridor, it's like having a personal sage or guru on tap 24 hours a day.

Someone you can go to in times of crisis and confusion. A guru who will give you clear considered and practical advice that's guaranteed to help relieve your problem and take away your anxiety and frustration. You get this by having clarity of purpose, and knowing where you're going. Once you've put a stake in the ground to say this is where I am and this is where I'm going, you have a starting point of reference, almost like your own global positioning satellite system.

Think about where you are and where you're heading and try constructing your own corridor (see Figure 20):

Figure 20 *Your decision corridor*

Once you've thought about what you will and won't do, think about the degree of control you have over those factors. Although there are things you're not prepared to do, can you really say no? Is there a degree of emotional or financial liability to consider, such that you have to abide by someone else's choices? Debt, both moral and financial, often constrains our actions.

So for these choices that you would like to make but can't at the moment because of personal commitment or other liabilities, redraw the corridor, but this time put a time line along the bottom as in Figure 21.

By using the timeline decision corridor you can define what is important now and what might be important in the future. This will help build a richer picture of where you're going and what the

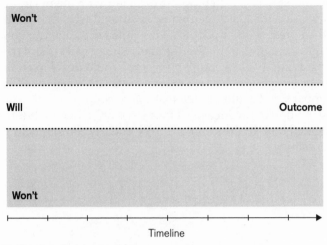

Figure 21 *Timeline decision corridor*

critical factors are along the way. It might be that some of the 'will's and 'won't's are only aspirations at the moment, but at least they are on the table for you to consider and share with those around you. The final stage in this journey is to take one of the things you wish to achieve, and then ask yourself: How can I make this even better? Take some time to consider your own case.

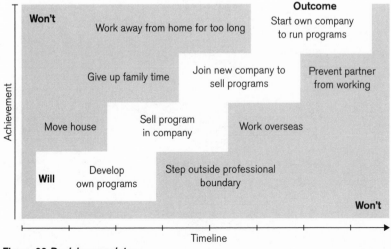

Figure 22 *Decision escalator*

As an example, you can step up the escalator with me in Figure 22. When I worked for a large company, I wanted to develop programs rather than present other people's ideas; the next stage was to work within the company, running programs where I had control over the content; leaving to join a company where I could develop and run my own products was the next move; and finally, I left to set up my own company so I could maintain absolute control over the quality and distribution of my ideas. All four steps are different, but they are underpinned both by freedom of choice and my commitment to be with my family.

Chunk up

It makes sense to plan your escalator ride, but it can be difficult to think about what the upper-level outcomes might be. If you only see the world from the bottom rung of the escalator then it can be difficult to set stretching goals. It makes more sense to rise above the current position to get a bird's eye view of the opportunities and threats that await you on your journey. You won't be surprised to hear this, but it isn't easy. The first step is to step inside out – step back and get a clearer view of who you are and what life looks like from a different perspective. Figure 23 shows how it can help to chunk up and enhance your current map of the world.

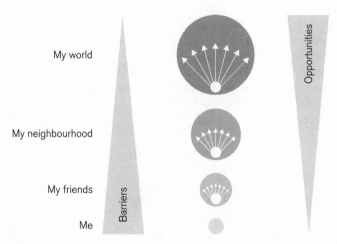

Figure 23 *Chunking up*

At the lowest level, look at the world from your perspective. Describe your current situation in terms of your assets, liabilities, opportunities and barriers from a subjective position. What will happen if you step inside out and describe how your position looks to your friends, family and work colleagues? Some of them might suggest that some of the barriers you perceive are only minor or of your own making. They might be able to expand some of your perceived opportunities by suggesting how your personal capital can be applied in a different way. Now chunk this up again and look at your situation from the viewpoint of the people in your neighbourhood. This might be the mayor, priest, rabbi or anyone who is able to look at your position as one person existing within a community of ten or twenty thousand people. Again, it might be that your whole situation can be described in a totally different way, with new frames on the barriers and opportunities.

Finally, now step back and see the situation from a whole-world perspective. How would the US president or the queen of the Netherlands view your position? They would certainly offer a perspective that was not obvious from your position. If you're feeling adventurous, describe how a visitor from Mars might see your opportunities and barriers. How would they reframe your perspective to be more positive?

Just step yourself through the following questions and see if you can reframe your current situation.

- How do I describe my situation?

- How would my friends describe my situation?

- How would the local religious or political leader describe my situation?

- How would the local paper describe my situation?

- How would national TV describe my situation?

- How would the government describe my situation?

- How would the UN Assembly describe my situation?

Ultimately, all descriptions can be broken down into good and bad; upside and downside; opportunities and barriers. Look at the spin that different newspapers put on the same story – it's either negative or positive according to their own agenda.

So, when you describe your current position, it's important to look at the upside and the downside from your position and from the position of others involved in your life.

For example, imagine you're in a job where you've been performing really well and believe that the next promotion should be yours. But the company decides to employ someone from outside the company. At that moment you feel angry, frustrated and upset with the way you've been treated. Your first thoughts are to tell the company what to do with their job and to start looking elsewhere. However, if you can chunk up and look at the bigger picture, you might be able to learn and benefit from the experience. Step into the senior team's role and look at the company performance; talk with friends in other companies to understand how they view your company; look at what's happening in the market where your company operates. With this broad view of the world you might start to understand that the business needs to enter new markets and must make this shift in the next six months. Because of this strategic shift the business had to pull in outside experience and ideas. But you now have new insight and a clearer appreciation of the market the company wants to enter, and from this you can develop a new goal. Talk with your newly appointed colleague, read different journals, increase your social network and broaden your access to market information.

By stepping outside of your world and viewing where you are and what to be from a different perspective you'll be better prepared to realize your potential.

Far too many people say they know where they're going, but have embarked on a journey that has in-built limitations. Their route is limited because it has been mapped by someone else; or was planned with only limited understanding of the world outside; or it was undertaken by the insecure part of you. The 'know where you're going' decision is fundamentally about stretching your boundaries to reach new parts, not to carry on the way you always have. The goal of any leadership journey must be to realize all the latent and innate potential that you have at your command.

Failure to release your true personal potential is a failure to lead yourself.

Turn on the potential tap

As you read this book, there will be an inner voice commenting on the ideas, the models, and my typing errors. The voice offers a running commentary on what you're reading and how you think and feel about it, and tries to steer your head and heart in certain directions. In many cases, the inner voice is a powerful tool that helps you fight imaginary monsters or talk yourself through emotional traumas. However, it can also be a tremendously powerful force that prevents you from making real headway in your personal plans. This blocking energy comes from the insecurity driver. This is the part of the heart dimension that believes with absolute passion that there are things in life that you can't do, that will hurt you or that don't make sense. The insecurity driver pushes you to get satisfaction from the things that you know and from others' answers, rather than taking risks yourself.

You just know you're going to miss it this time!
Think about a sport you play. Most of the time you happily take part in the game and are satisfied with the outcome. But there is probably a certain ball you find difficult to play or a particular player you don't get along with. And every time this thing crops up, your inner voice reminds you. Your inner voice is the little devil in disguise that acts as a potential tap. It's just a tiny voice, but it has the potential to prevent you from releasing the wealth of talent stored in your personal reservoir. However, there are examples of people who have learned to control this inner voice and manage to keep it in line; as a result, they generate more freedom and personal power.

One of the most inspiring stories for me has been Christopher Reeve. In a TV interview, Sir David Frost talked with him about the difficulties he faces every day, and asked how he deals with the shock of not being able to move. Christopher Reeve answered:

I get busy and readjust and focus on what can I do today. There is a phrase that I use which is 'bad days are good days in disguise'. You can start out feeling pretty miserable about the injustice of it all. The way out is to think of something that needs doing and there is always something that will take you forward, and I just focus on that and I get back in shape.

This 'know where you're going' outcome isn't a one-, two- or three-year objective (although that might underpin the overall motivation). Christopher Reeve has to set a new personal outcome the moment he wakes up. He uses this driving force to help him survive the emotional and physical torture he experiences daily. By developing this inner mantra, he uses his *in*-security to overpower the insecurity and is able to prevent negative behaviour from emerging.

The problem is that when trying to define and plan where you're going, the inner voice can set up a raging torrent of critique, all aimed at stopping you from experiencing things that are new and challenging. It might be doing this to protect you, but sometimes it can be wrong. You have to learn to manage it.

'Manage' doesn't mean ignore or overcome.

If you fight it, much of your emotional and intellectual energy is being forced into your internal space, and energy that should be focused on making a change is lost. The trick is to come up with a question to ask the voice. After all, the tap is there to protect you from harm. Like the release valve on a steamer or the governor on an engine, it's being protective in its own way. Rather than fighting the inner voice, set up a series of internal challenges or dialogues. The next time you feel the tap being closed off by the inner voice, ask yourself these questions:

◆ What would it be like if I went ahead?

◆ What's the worst thing that could happen?

◆ What would I do if I weren't afraid?

◆ Has anyone else ever done it? What harm came to them?

By using this approach, you're harnessing the intellectual power of the head dimension to challenge some of the fears offered by the insecure part of the heart dimension. By asking these two dimensions to argue their case, it can become possible to overcome irrational fears stimulated by the insecurity driver. It's also important to recognize that, although the logic of the question and argument comes from the head dimension, the energy and passion for this must come from the *in*-security drive in the heart dimension.

At the end of the day, the heart dimension controls the potential tap, and it's this function that controls the release of your potential. Therefore it's important that you understand the importance of the choose-your-choice component. Unless you accept that you have the right, power and energy to manage your internal voices and choices, then all of these words will have little impact.

You just know you're going to hit it this time
The first challenge to test for yourself might be to think of one thing that you've always said you can't do.

Take this thing that the voice says you can't do and work through the questions shown in Figure 24. If they don't fit the issue exactly then bend and shape them to make sense. The primary purpose is to help

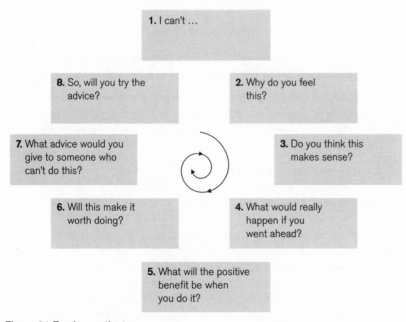

Figure 24 *Turning on the tap*

your head component and the *in*-security driver to reframe the issue to help the heart understand that it isn't dangerous or life threatening. If you do a single loop and your heart's answer is still no but the objective has shifted, then circulate again basing your questions on the new objective. Loop as many times as you need to in order to get to a point where your heart is prepared to give it a shot.

- ◆ **I can't ...** Think of something you feel you're unable to do. It might be dealing with a problem at work or challenging someone who seems intolerant. Try to focus on something that you know is possible but which seems to have some reason why you can't do it.

- ◆ **Why do you feel this?** What internal insecurity forces cause you to believe you can't do something? Have you a legacy experience? Or has someone else fed you their fantasy that it's difficult to do?

- ◆ **Do you think this makes sense?** From a logical perspective why is it a barrier? Is there a sensible reason why you don't want to do it?

- ◆ **What would really happen if you went ahead?** Just supposing that you did take action, what would happen? What is the worst that could happen? And what is the best?

- ◆ **What will the positive benefit be when you do it?** Imagine you've taken action. How will your life improve? How will it be better for others and how will this feel for you?

- ◆ **Will this make it worth doing?** Do the benefits outweigh the pain of making the change? What personal benefits will accrue for you?

- ◆ **What advice would you give to someone who can't do this?** Step outside your situation. What advice would you give to someone else who is in a similar situation? How would you help them to help themselves?

- ◆ **So, will you try the advice?** Would you take your own advice and overcome that initial, self-created barrier? When will you effect the change? What's the next barrier you would like to overcome?

To really know where you're going, you need to understand your self-imposed limitations and work out ways to overcome them. If you do what you always did, you will get what you always got. Unless you really believe that you have your personal leadership in place and don't need to change, you will benefit by changing your entrenched ideas and habits. Even if you believe that you don't need to change how you operate, it will pay to challenge that assumption!

Personal leadership inventory

Having established your destination, you need to understand the attributes and resources you'll use to get there. The personal leadership inventory (PLI) is a simple but effective way to understand what you have going for you and what changes you need to make to help realize your dreams.

To complete the PLI, first list all the resources you use to manage your life. Then consider the level of control you have around each one. The maths is easy. If you feel that you do have absolute freedom of choice, give yourself a score of 10. If you feel that it is shared choice, give yourself a score of 5 and if you don't believe that you have the freedom to make a choice, then use a score of 0. If you decide your response falls in between, allocate your score accordingly.

Inventory	Score

Who I am
Describe you as a person – not in terms of what you do – but what is important to you and what your purpose is and what value you offer to the world.

To what extent are you able to change the real you at will?

What I do
Income generation: How do you earn a living and what do you take to market? This might be as a full-time job or it might be a hobby that you could turn into a marketable asset.

To what extent do you choose your income?

Who with

Executive directors: people who are directly involved in your life and play a significant role in how you make decisions, for example, your wife, husband, partner or business associates.

What degree of influence do they have over the choices you make?

Non-exec directors: people who offer you advice but don't have a direct link into how you live, for example, your manager, parent or tutor. Just how much value do you place on their counsel? What would be the impact it they ceased to offer advice or guidance? Would this disrupt your life?

What degree of influence do they have over the choices you make?

Associates: people with whom you have an equal stake and share assets or activities. It might be co-partners in a business or members of the family. In this relationship you might share decisions about common topics or shared assets.

What degree of influence do they have over the choices you make?

Stakeholders: people who have a vested interest in your personal performance but might not have control over your choices. This might be team members, neighbours, or peers. What level of influence do they try to exert over the choices you make?

What degree of influence do they have over the choices you make?

Dependants: people not directly involved with you but who will be impacted upon if you change anything. What level of responsibly do you feel for them? Has this impacted on choices you've made in your life?

What degree of influence do they have over the choices you make?

Assets

Financial: assets such as savings, pensions, etc. Do you have instant access or is there a delay in using the funds? Does anyone have control over your financial assets?

To what extent does this influence the choices you make?

Brand: What is your value as a brand? Your market capitalization is wholly dependent upon how much other people value your worth. Do you know how much other people value you? Do you have a clear proposition that you offer to others and are they clear as to what it is? Who is your primary competitor? What control do they have over the market you operate in?

To what extent does this influence the choices you make?

Network: What is the strength and deployment of your personal network? How many people do you know who can and will support you in any changes you might wish to make? What would happen if they choose not to stay within your network, how will that impact on your life and income?

To what extent does this influence the choices you make?

Liabilities

Financial debt: What extent of short- and long-term debts, such as loans, mortgage, store cards, do you have? How does this impact on your freedom to make decisions? How quickly can you redeem loans? And do you have a plan in place to do so?

To what extent does this influence the choices you make?

Emotional debt: Are there people you feel obliged to and who have a call on your time and energy? Where has the debt come from and can it be redeemed? Do such debts prevent you from making choices?

To what extent does this influence the choices you make?

Legacy: anything in your background that might cause a problem if you were to make a significant change in your life direction. This might be an old story, or mistakes that prevent you from taking certain decisions.

To what extent does this influence the choices you make?

Total score (130 maximum)

Score of 100–130
You have a high level of choice and control in your life. But beware, such a high control factor might lead to a position where you could be perceived as a selfish leader.

Score of 40–99
You have some choice but a degree of your life is under the control of someone else. You might decide to go back to the questions and consider the areas where you've given away your choice. Is it choice that you're happy to trade away, or would you like to regain some of the choice options?

heart

lead yourself

momentum

0–39
You've given up a fair percentage of your ability to manage choice in your life. You might want to get some of it back.

For each of the sections in the inventory, ask yourself: Do I really have control over this section? If I wanted to, could I change this today, or are there other factors that prevent or hinder the process?

For example, if you list a number of people as stakeholders in your life (colleagues or peers) can you really choose to change that structure or is there a financial or emotional contract that means you must negotiate change?

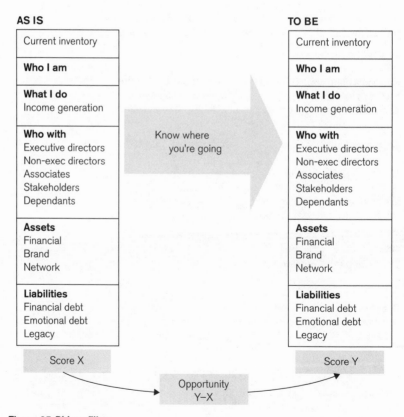

Figure 25 *PLI profiling*

If you consider that the first pass of the PLI completion is the 'AS IS' measurement, now complete the PLI again as a 'TO BE' rating (Figure 25). Indicate the rating you'd like to have for each section in a perfect world. By comparing the final score you'll get a feel for the choice gap in your life. If there's a large gap, then maybe you have less control over your direction than you think.

To help build the 'TO BE' PLI, step outside your current world view and really force yourself to step into the future. Just imagine your perfect day. If you could describe the world, as you'd like it to be, how would you describe who you are, what you'd do and who you'd do it with? In a perfect world what assets and liabilities would you have? Don't limit yourself to the current world view that you operate from. Use the following ideas to cajole yourself into designing a brave new world for yourself and the people in your life:

◆ Write your version of Martin Luther King's 'I have a dream' speech – what is your fantasy?

◆ What are your deep values? How can they be satisfied and nurtured?

◆ What is your end game? What would your epitaph say?

◆ How would your friends describe your life and your contribution to their lives?

◆ What big choices do you want to have made in one, three and five years' time? What resources will you need to make them?

◆ What choices do you plan to give to others? How will this impact on your future state?

◆ What are the things you're prepared to do in the future, and what are things you want to say no to?

◆ What things would you place on the decision escalator, and by what degree will they improve and when?

◆ Step up and see how the community would like to view your future: what good things do they see in you?

◆ Be conscious of who you want to be and separate this from who you want to belong to: what associations do you want to have and which do you choose not to be part of?

- If you turned on your potential tap fully, what would come out?
- What would friends and colleagues say would come out if the potential tap were opened fully?
- What are the insecurity drivers that restrict your movement forward?
- What are the *in*-security drivers that will help you to move forward?
- How can you use your head dimension to make logical and rational choices about your future position?
- If you could do any one thing differently, what would it be?

The aim with all these questions is to build yourself a framework of the future that you can use today to understand what decisions you need to make now. If we don't make decisions that help us achieve a real future, we risk taking choices that only lead to failure and misery.

Avoid crashing at bluffers' bend

A word of warning. I've seen so many people going through their planning process who come out with wild statements that bear little resemblance to what they are or what they might be. The rule is to be true to yourself and be true to others. Don't think you can go for gold in the high jump at the Olympics if you're 30 years old and 18 stone. You might be willing to try, but the drain on your life would be quite devastating. There is little joy in seeing someone giving everything up to achieve an impossible dream. The heart will let you fly but the head will always ensure you don't have a bumpy landing.

While hope plays a great part in our lives, realism often takes over to keep pain and misery to a minimum; having outlandish expectations can be emotionally destructive, especially for our loved ones.

And be genuine with others. Falsifying your future will destroy your credibility and, even worse, can destroy the good will and trust that you need to call on in order to achieve your true goals in life.

Outcome testing

Many people begin a self-improvement transformation, but not all of them stick with it. They might manage a change in the way they lead themselves and others, but it's often short-lived because the pull of the past is too strong. Ask yourself now, as you've come this far: Do I really have the will power and desire to hold on to my new personal leadership style and not revert to my old ways? Myself, I can answer, yes, of course I have. But I'm sitting here in Cyprus by the pool typing up the pages of this book. Who knows what will happen once I get back home and the daily grind starts again?

But there is one tool I use to test resolve, and that's the OUTCOME model.

This is a simple yet powerful set of questions that highlights whether a person will stick with it or whether it's just another new year's resolution.

Think about one single change you want to make as a result of reading this or any other book. Put it into words so that you can write in the box below (like this: I will do xxx by xx/xx/xx).

I will

_____

_____

by

_____

Now answer the following questions. Don't think about them, just give your instant gut reaction.

Question	Response
Is this change within your control, namely, do you have all the necessary resources, finances and time to make it happen?	
Are you sure that no one else can impact on your ability to make this happen?	
Are you clear why you want to make the change?	
Do you think that you're totally motivated and committed to delivering this by the date you've stated?	
In making this change are you clear as to what you'll have to give up (personal time, money, time with family, freedom, etc.)?	
Are you happy to lose this in exchange for the benefits gained from making the change?	
Can you describe how life will be different once the change is in place, namely, how you'll think, feel and behave differently?	
Can you describe how life in general will be different for you once the change is made?	
Can you describe all the people who will be affected by your change?	
Are you happy that your change doesn't unduly impact on the life of any one else?	
Can the change be measured?	
Have you put measures in place to ensure the outcome is achieved?	
What is the first step that you'll have to take to deliver the change?	
Is there something you can do right now?	

Now look back at your responses. Look at how many times you answered 'yes', 'no' and 'not sure'. Where you have 'no' and 'not sure', go back to the question and ask it again. See if you can think it through a bit more and, honestly, transform it to a 'yes'. There's no hard and fast rule about this technique, but in general the more you answer 'no' and 'not sure', the less likely it is that you'll actually deliver on the promise you've made to yourself.

Each of the questions tests a separate function of the OUTCOME model. It challenges the extent to which you've really considered the emotional, behavioural and logical factors that underpin and reinforce personal change, and is built around the following structure.

◆ **Own:** *Who owns the outcome, and is it self-maintained?* Ultimately, the question is, do you have the desire and capability to change your leadership style or will other external factors prevent you from taking the necessary actions? Do you hold all the levers (financial, time, resources, etc.), or are you dependent on others to help make the shift forward?

◆ **Unease:** *What triggered the need for change?* Why do you need to improve how you lead yourself? Is there real motivation behind the change in style? A casual decision to make a change can lead to constant failure that in turn diminishes your appetite and motivation to effect real personal change. Aim high but be realistic, and give yourself the best shot at it.

◆ **Trade-offs:** *What will you have to give up in order to achieve your change?* One often-forgotten fact is that we adopt certain behaviours because there is a payback. Delivering a new personal leadership style means that something will change, but something will also be lost. You must think through and appreciate the potential loss before you commit to any new personal strategy.

◆ **Change:** *How will life be different when your change is made?* Test the value of your new way of thinking, feeling and behaving by clarifying what new value will be created. Take a mental step forward – consider how life will be different at the end of the improvement. Imagine what language will be used, what the environment will look like, what your personal improvement will be.

◆ **Others:** *What impact will it have on others?* In effecting a new personal strategy, one of the dangers is that short-term and urgent forces are being responded to and little attention is paid to the impact that the change will be having on other people. It's important to consider all the people that are affected by any change you make. One way is to consider them in terms of winners, losers or neutrals. You'll be able to create a realistic picture of who will be affected by the proposed change and, more importantly, how they will be affected.

- ◆ **Measuring:** *How will the change be measured?* How will you know if your change has been successful? To be certain that the strategy is one you really want and can achieve, you need to be able to describe in simple terms how you'll know that your leadership style has improved.

- ◆ **Engage:** *What is the first step?* The hardest part in any personal strategy is the first step or the point of engagement. Procrastination is the enemy of personal change. Therefore at this point, say what your first action will be. What will you do right now – not later today or tomorrow?

So, now you have your goal, and you're clear about the impact, the implications and the requirements of getting there.

Know where you're going: quick summary

◆ You have three aspects to your life: the way you behave – the part others see; the way you think – the rational part of you; the way you feel – your secret inner life that only you know. When these are separated, you feel confused or anxious; when aligned, you gain a clear sense of purpose.

◆ Problems occur when you: say you'll take one journey but want to take another; don't know what journey you want to take; take opposing journeys to those with whom you work or live.

◆ Having a clear sense of where you're heading ensures that the choices you make today will be of value tomorrow.

◆ Who you are and what you do are two very different entities – join them at your peril. Don't become so dependent on a person or group that they become your primary source of personal power or income.

◆ Imagine what you'd be able to achieve if you weren't afraid of that first step. Challenge the inner voice that's blocking your potential tap. Move from 'I can't' to 'I can'.

◆ Map your personal inventory so you understand where your strengths and weaknesses are and how they can best be deployed.

◆ Avoid the new year's resolution situation where personal promises fail to materialize – define where you're going and ensure you have the will and capability to get there.

head
enlarging the map

Variety's the very spice of life
That gives it all its flavour.

William Cowper

The head holds the map for your journey. The head dimension offers a rational view of the world and is the guiding voice of calm and reason when the heart is in control.

Think about where you are at the moment. Are you able to step back and take a view of the world as it is rather than how you think you see it? Do you see other people's points of view and accept them as reasonable? Are you able to change how you change rather than just steam-rolling your way through life?

Your answers to these questions tell us the extent to which the head function is playing a role in your life, how much you're able to manage your life, and how you change your life according to a variety of rules, not taking just the single-track heart-led approach.

The heart says, 'I know where I'm going and I'm going to get there by hook or by crook.' The head says, 'Fine, but let's make sure we actually make it in one piece so it's a really effective journey.' To do this the head needs to have breadth of choice. It needs to be able to call on a range of views and ideas to ensure the direction set by the heart is achieved, though it won't necessarily be by the route the heart had envisaged.

Imagine you're on the way to work and you suddenly run into a huge traffic jam. You're probably late, the client is ready to sign the contract and you were late for the last meeting so you can't afford to let her down this time. You're flustered, worried and tense. You start to imagine all the worst things that might possibly happen: you'll lose the contract, which means your pay rise will be cut, which means reduced income this year, which means, oh no! you can't afford to pay for the holiday you booked two months ago. It could become quite a long list ...

In this situation, though, the head dimension can help. It can talk to the heart and say, 'Why not call the office and see if anyone knows a way to bypass the hold-up? Or ring in to see where the client lives? She might be sitting in the same traffic jam. What about calling the client to explain the problem and see if any work can be done on the phone in the car?' The head has to generate as wide a range of options as possible because, if it can only offer the same old solutions that the heart has already considered, its help will be rejected and the emotional trauma will continue.

If the head can cast a wide net and find totally new ideas, the heart will be affected by the head's rational input and will start to listen and respond.

Rich variety: get spoilt for choice

We need to have sufficient variety to generate new ideas, thoughts and solutions that will enhance our capability to lead ourself and others. It's known as Ashby's law of requisite variety. Ashby suggested that any regulator must have as much or more variety than the system it regulates. In a game of chess, the variety of moves you have available must be greater than the variety of moves available to your opponent. The same can be seen in football, the stock market, a children's painting competition. In any situation, you have to understand how much choice and variety exists, and then be able to match or exceed this level. The person with the most flexibility will influence and lead the environment.

Think back to when you were a child, desperate for the latest toy. You wanted it bad. It was the most important thing in the world. But your mum said no, so you went to your dad. He in turn said no, so you pressured your grandparents and favourite aunties and uncles. After this failed to work you adopted different strategies: sulking, sobbing, screaming, and scratching the brand new furniture. This went on and on until your strategies worked. Even though the grown-ups tried to respond to all your strategies with their own responses, ultimately you outdid them. You had the staying power to try more and more ways to get want you wanted from them. As a parent, there are only so many punishments you can invoke, but as a child the options available are mind blowing. At this point both you and your parents experienced the awesome power of rich variety.

Your persistence can be summarized as 'if what you're doing doesn't work, do something else'. The head dimension uses this as its primary ethos and argues that we must increase the variety in the ways we lead ourselves and others. We use the variety in two ways. First, use the diversity to see life from more than just a unitary standpoint. Second, life is movement and movement is change. If we are to change ourselves and others successfully, we must learn how to map our maps and change how we change.

To enhance your personal leadership you have to look beyond the standard solutions and learn how to originate new ideas and alternatives. The person who only has restricted variety in their armoury will fall by the wayside as other competitors come along and offer more diverse, rich and imaginative solutions.

You need to operate from the rich variety perspective to match environmental needs and become a more successful leader.

Restricted variety

So, how do we know when a person, team or organization has a restrictive mental map? Think of the typical political interview. The pattern is generally consistent. The politician is asked a question by the interviewer and promptly responds with a pre-planned monologue of what they believe is right or wrong about the current situation. The answer might well be very interesting, but the interviewer wants to broaden the discussion, so asks another question. The politician responds but gives pretty much the same information as before, perhaps framed slightly differently. So the charade goes on, with the interviewer in the guise of attacker and the guest acting as valiant defender, persistently rehashing the same idea again and again.

Whenever human beings come together in a group, they instinctively create a framework for restrictive variety.

If you accept the premise that maximized variety is better than minimized variety, ask yourself why we don't do more of it.

In its natural state, the world is a cauldron of natural richness and variety. In their natural state, human beings are infinitely variable – two people are never totally the same. Put these two sets of variables together and we have a world that is complex and chaotic. To survive in this world we have to filter out a great deal of randomness and create mental maps that bring order and common sense into our lives. In effect, we choose the degree of variety required to make life liveable. As we are continually trying to bring order into our lives by restricting the variety we face, when we form into groups or make associations, the restrictive process is compounded.

The average level of mediocrity! (ALOM)

This norming or restricting of options and choices results in the average level of mediocrity. Put together a football team of highly talented players, and the restrictive factors actually clash and constrain the talent within the group. So one player's preferred style might be to run down the wing and cross a high ball for someone to head in from inside the box, while the center-forward's preference is to avoid heading the ball, preferring to work through the back line with one-on-one tackling.

The football manager's role is partly about getting skilled players into the team but, more importantly, being able to recognize where restrictive forces will reduce the overall effectiveness of the team.

You cannot be serious!
The ALOM effect can be seen in any situation where two or more people come together. In an organization, it will be evident in everything the organization says and does. Every time it puts in a new process or system it imposes the mental map of the designer on the organization and those using the system, and prevents them from using their own unique thoughts, feelings and behaviours. The leader's view of the world places you in a position of restricted behaviour.

Take any system, process, standard, project methodology. They all limit and constrain the level of variety. But with good reason – any business that wants to deliver the right product, to the right person, at the right time, at the right cost, must control its processes to maintain consistency. However, controls over the way the business behaves shouldn't mean that they restrict the way people feel and think.

Think about your current work team. Write their names below and picture each person in turn. Think about all their potential, market value and what they are really capable of. Now think what the same person might be capable of with just a small amount of coaching and development. In column A place a number that indicates their potential – use 10 as the highest market value down to 1 for someone who isn't really capable of creating high value in the market.

Name	A	B
1		
2		
3		
4		
5		

In column B, rate their effectiveness in a team event. What value do they bring to the room? To what extent does their contribution make a difference?

Wherever B has a lower rating than A, ask yourself why. What happens to reduce the effectiveness of the person and, importantly, how does that limit the whole team's overall value or output? The reduction in group output leads to the ALOM effect, where the unique potential that each person brings to the room is deflated and defeated by the group effort to maintain sensibility and norms. On one hand we want to bring people together to realize a collaborative output, but the end result is often the opposite.

Now, I'm not about to suggest that we should start a revolution, turn the clock back and abolish the whole idea of the firm. But we must be very careful whenever we bring teams together to create value. Like the football team manager, it's essential to be vigilant about overcoming and eliminating such restrictions.

Two ways to achieve this are, firstly, to help people explore the maps they use to manage their world and generate their abilities to rebuild and reframe their views. Secondly, wherever possible, challenge people to change how they manage the process of change. If the group has made a decision to do something, question how they plan to deliver the outcome and encourage them to consider alternative ways to manage the process and achieve the same.

Release the giant within
The strange thing about ALOM is that it's not something obvious that you notice when you walk into an organization. As a consultant I can visit an organization and the president will proudly tell me of their work rate, staff survey records and key performance measures. This tells me what they are doing well, but it doesn't tell me what they could be doing better. Whenever I consult with a company I always try to ask one simple question. 'On a scale of 10 [10 being the most positive] to what degree does the organization unleash and tap into the potential of its people?' The average score is between 3 and 5. In some cases I get a 7, but in others it drops to 0 and 1. When I ask this question, it isn't just to the workers and frontline operators, I ask the same question throughout the business, and the result is consistent, even in companies known to be innovative leaders in work style and performance.

In order to lead others effectively you must have the ability to unleash the latent and innate talent that lies untouched throughout most people's working lives.

Don't let your team members be like Marlon Brando in *On the Waterfront*: 'I could have been a contender.' Personal leadership is about never saying 'I could have ... ', it's about saying 'I have'.

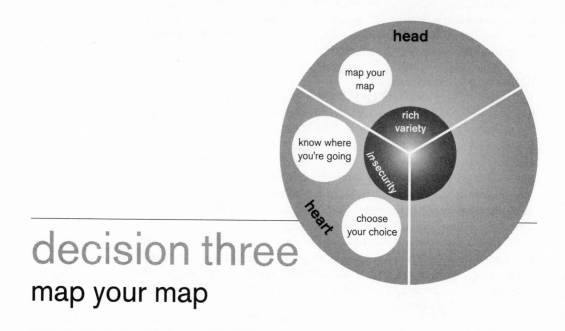

decision three
map your map

The man who views the world at 50 the same as he did at 20 has wasted 30 years of his life.

Muhammad Ali

Your plane is coming in to land at Heathrow airport, and suddenly the pilot announces that the undercarriage is stuck and the plane will have to make an emergency landing. When the plane lands, you're instructed to leave the plane rapidly, as a fire may break out. Do you leave quickly and safely as instructed, or, as is the reality in many crashes, do you put your life at risk by waiting to get your things out of the overhead luggage rack?

Most people still follow the mental map programmed for a normal landing. The standard map is, on landing, everyone stands up and waits to get their possessions, and only once this task is achieved do they leave the plane. But in an emergency, speed is of the essence, and the quickest person out of the plane has the greatest chance of survival. Evidence suggests that those who survive are the people who ignore the existing map of self-imposed rules, and look for ways to circumvent the normal landing procedures.

In this section, we'll look at the following:

◆ **Clean the lens.** We all get used to one view of the world and sometimes we can't see the wood for the trees. But we need to consider how we find a fresh outlook.

◆ **Map shift.** The world moves on at such a pace that we need to discard our old view and take on board a whole new set of feelings, thoughts and behaviours.

◆ **Shadow maps.** Behind every map sits another, the ones that people don't talk about and keep locked away only ever to be shared with the people they trust. We have to unlock these maps; without them, it's too easy to take a wrong turn and end up not knowing where we're going.

◆ **Map conflict.** In the main, conflict doesn't occur because of a problem, it's just that two people are viewing the same situation from a different perspective. Build a bridge between the two maps and the potential for conflict is reduced.

◆ **Fantasy league.** Our mental maps are not rigid and they become distorted over time. What appears to be the truth or a correct decision one day might seem totally different another day. This distortion happens as we turn fact into fantasy through inference.

◆ **Map expansion.** One way to enrich your map is to explore other people's maps. As the two views contrast, conflict and coalesce, you can create a new view of the world that is unique and full of possibilities.

Clean the lens

The ability to modify how you map the world is your key to survival.

Imagine you're in the Australian outback with a temperature hovering around 40°C. All you see is a blistering landscape that seems barren and devoid of food or drink. To the untrained eye it looks like a desert, but to the Aborigine it's a rich opportunity to harvest food and water: the seeds from sparse clumps of Wollybutt grass make flour; the seeds from the acacia tree are like peas; and the bottle-shaped yellow blossoms from the Corkwood tree can be beaten against the palm to produce sweet nectar that has a smoked honey flavour. Remapping your world is a key to survival.

The ability to rebuild your map is an essential characteristic of leaders and innovators. They are able to take a distorted view of the world and from this create new products and ideas around the world. Masaru Ibuka, Sony's Honorary Chairman, conceived of the notion of the Walkman, a product that has gone on to sell millions around the world; and Trevor Bayliss dreamed up the idea of the clockwork radio. Richard Branson continues to break existing map structures, always stretching the portfolio one step further. We have yet to see if Virgin Galactic, his hotels in space, will succeed, but his visionary ability shows an extraordinary ability to remap his map of the journey.

Your mental map is the framework that guides how you think, feel and behave.

Map shift

The root of all leadership and learning is the map shift.

Where an individual has to be prepared to discard or throw away the current world view and accept an alternative frame of reference. In making this shift, the self-sustaining loop must be broken. This loop is a common process; people see the world in a particular way, and so expect it to behave according to the criteria set out in their own particular mental map. For you to change yourself or others you must create a break in the current pattern and force a shift to a new way of thinking (see Figure 26).

Once the world is seen in a new way, the shift can be used to reinforce this new world position. However, this can soon drift towards the negative. If you decide to stop at that point, and don't use the experience to energize further map shifts, then the change or learning will only be of limited value.

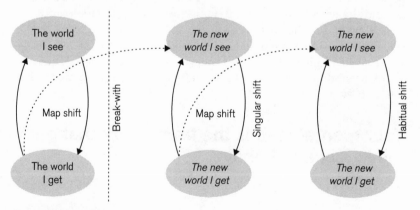

Figure 26 *Map shift*

Failure to change mapping rarely has extreme consequences but the failure of the commanding officers to accept that the invasion of Singapore in 1941 would occur at the site where it did resulted in the death of thousands of people. Defences were designed on the assumption that any invasion would be sea-based and would come from the southern side of the island. As a result, the northern shore was left undefended. Although the local plantation owners, who understood the Malay Peninsula and the Japanese people, repeatedly highlighted the risk of attack from the north, they were overruled or ignored by the commanding forces. And even when Japanese transports were sighted off the southern tip of Indo-China, the potential for a northern attack was negated.

The problem was rooted in the fact that the guardians of Singapore could not risk allow themselves to be wrong and routinely issued communiqués to the people of Singapore denying that a problem existed. Only in 1948 did General Wavell admit to the governor of Singapore that the fault for the lack of preparation must be placed on the heads of the military. You can see how the cause of the problem must have arisen from an inability and unwillingness amongst the leaders to free themselves of entrenched ways of thinking and accept that alternatives might be available.

Once you break with the past, you can create the future you desire, and the idea of true personal leadership, where you control your own life, can start to emerge. First you learn to understand the boundaries we all operate to and then you begin to understand how to stretch your own boundaries every day. We all have personal limitations that are imposed by us, by external factors, or jointly. These are the maps that we operate to. If I have a map of the London Underground, I can find my way around London by tube; if I have a map of the world, my choice is boundless.

Shadow maps

In *Peter Pan*, there is the idea that people have detachable shadows, parts of themselves that can be removed and sewn back on. In reality we often have two aspects to our personalities: open maps and shadow maps. The trouble is that shadow maps can't be detached, so they have to work in conjunction with the open maps. This tension can create problems and blockages in our learning process as we develop and manage our relationships.

Everyone has their own two maps: the open map relates to things we are comfortable with and happy to share with others; and the shadow map relates to the hidden or concealed areas – those behaviours, thoughts and feelings that we are less comfortable sharing. The shadow map is all the important activities and arrangements that don't get identified, discussed and managed in relationships that are important to us.

The existence of shadow maps causes us to establish defence routines to protect ourselves from embarrassment or surprise. Defence routines exist; they are undiscussable, but they help us deal with embarrassment or threat. By tacitly following the four rules in Figure 27, people inherently lock themselves into certain behaviours.

Meeting (*shadow*) ground rules

1. Bypass embarrassment or threat whenever possible.
2. Act as if you are not bypassing them.
3. Do not discuss 1 or 2 while it is happening.
4. Do not discuss the undiscussability of the undiscussable.

Figure 27 *Shadow ground rules*

Problems surface if someone decides to tackle any of the rules head-on, asking people to clarify what the problem is, trying to discuss some of the deeper issues in the office, or raising problems that people don't want to talk about. All of these are likely to trigger some form of defensive reaction. The problem for us is how to avoid this defensive reply and the resulting strangulation or corruption of a sound relationship.

Christopher Argyris suggests that the shadow map deals with the covert, the undiscussed, undiscussable and the unmentionable. These all sit in the shade of the person or organization, and only appear when a light is deliberately shone on them. He suggests that an organization's true patterns of activity are frequently incongruous with the espoused theories contained in their formal business documents, such as organization charts, policy statements and job descriptions.

Consider a manager who joins a new company. She is slowly being introduced to the local systems and practices. In reading the in-house company papers, she is pleased to notice that the company is registered to a formal quality system and all the notice boards and paper work support its use. This is further reinforced by the files that exist in everyone's office on quality standards and local procedures. However, the files are never used, and people don't follow the system. Even worse, when she tries to adhere to the processes laid out in the files, she's ribbed by her colleagues and fails to make any headway with her work. After a while, she starts to watch what other people are doing, and decides to follow local practice rather than what's laid down in the books. All seems fine until she is asked to attend a team quality review meeting with the local auditor and worries that her team will be penalized for failing to follow the processes. But, at the meeting she is shocked to find that all the team members tell the auditor how good the quality processes are, and how much more efficient the business is with them in place. She is left with some confusion over the gap between what people are doing and what they say they do.

In this case, people have established a shared shadow map to protect themselves from any embarrassment or surprise. The avoidance of the quality procedures is widespread, and this behaviour is clearly accepted throughout the organization. If challenged on this, the directors will say that the organization is adhering to the standards, although they might suspect that this is not necessarily true. And as the operations are running well, the directors are loath to lift any rocks to find out what is really happening. The team believes it's OK to ignore the standards because they assume that the directors don't really want them to be followed as it would slow down the production rate.

A gentle stalemate is reached where neither side raises the issue and there is a tacit agreement to let sleeping dogs lie.

Interestingly, under these conditions, people are likely to have both good and bad feelings about the situation. The positive factor is that both the directors and the team are pleased at not having to follow procedures that might be constraining. On the downside, there might be a sense of frustration in both camps. The directors might well feel that the team should follow the quality procedures, since they are part of the overall company management system. The team may be dissatisfied that the directors don't care enough about quality to ensure that the standards are enforced. Through these shared defensive routines, people are using great skill to carefully avoid the issue of quality and adherence to the standards. However, lies can only be lived so long and one day the truth might rear its head.

As organizations become increasingly interdependent, value chains are being created across companies. In this situation there is every chance that a customer might well start to look more closely at the supplier's quality system to confirm that it is operating as it should. When the realization comes that the company has been flouting the system for a long time, and the company is close to losing the contract, what will happen? Well, the witch hunt will no doubt begin: the search will be on to find the guilty party who failed to ensure that the systems were followed. Then people would adopt their best defence routines – convincing themselves and others that they really were using the system, and that it must have been someone else who created the problem. And finally, the auditor would probably get fired and a team of external assessors would be employed to build a new quality system for the company!

This is a prime example of the dominance of shadow maps where defence routines exist but they are undiscussable. They proliferate and grow underground. The social pollution is hard to identify until something blows up in people's faces, or the legacy of deceit is passed on to the team further down the value chain.

There is no simple answer to building a relationship with someone who is operating out of a shadow map. However, to make a start, you need to step out of your world view and understand what the other person is feeling, no matter how alien or bizarre it is to you.

In doing this, it becomes possible to understand what their personal needs are, and why they are operating out of the shadow map. Once you understand, you can develop strategies for moving the relationship to an open level.

Map conflict

But problems can arise when people 'believe' they are operating to the same map – whereas in reality they are worlds apart. Shortly after I met my wife, she was working away and had decided to stop at my cousin's house in a small village called Bourne End. Although Lin had visited the house a couple of times, both times I had driven us there. Anyway, she felt confident enough about getting there and, at the end of her day's work, drove off to Bourne End and started to look for my cousin's house. She drove around for ages but couldn't seem to spot any useful landmarks. After a while she called me up and I tried to give her directions over the phone. All seemed OK – she knew that she had to look for a garage and then the house was a short way down on the left-hand side. After another half an hour she called me again. She couldn't find it. Although I was trying to understand her problem, it was getting late and I was tired and (in so many words) just told her to open her eyes and look for it, after all there was only one garage in the village! Then, at last, after more heated phone calls, we realized she was in the wrong Bourne End!

So, I had been giving her directions based on my mental map, and she had been trying to apply them to the (totally mis-matched) territory in front of her.

Map gap
My own experience has taught me:

◆ We often make assumptions about the map we use in relation to the maps other people use – this can lead to map dissonance or a difference in your respective views of the world.

◆ It's easy to fall into the trap that the map *is* the territory – clearly, the map is a representation of a physical set of characteristics, not the actual thing.

◆ The power of positive thinking means nothing at all if you're in the wrong place.

In essence the gaps between what we see and what others see leads to map gap, a dissonance between our reality and someone else's. You know the situation: we both go to see a film. I come out saying how great it was, especially the bit where the spy jumped from one building to another in the howling winds. You say what a load of crap and how can a person jump 25 feet in torrential winds. We've both experienced the same event but *choose* to create alternative, and conflicting, maps.

The key word I use here is choose.

We've both experienced the same event, at the same time, in the same place, and you'd expect that we'd end up with the same inner descriptions. But this clearly didn't happen. What *does* happen is that we tend to choose to selectively filter the film through the maps we already have. I could have chosen to view the 25-foot jump as false and theatrical, but my map was one of: 'I'm here to enjoy myself and switch my head off for two hours. I don't want to analyze and compare things; I just want an emotional, thrilling experience.' Your map is probably more head based. You went to the movies for stimulation and were intuitively analyzing the film to see how it stacked up against reality. However, we both had choices about how we view the film. I could have gone with a different emotion in place, used a different map and had a totally different experience.

It's this inner choice that leads to shared decisions to build empires, pyramids and political systems. But it's the same inner choice that causes conflict. Look in any newspaper the world over and I guarantee that up to 50 per cent of the stories are based on the idea of map dissonance. Look at the story below pulled out of the *Guardian*.

head

lead yourself

momentum

'We're not political,' says Women's Institute; 'Yes, you are,' says Downing Street

The ladies of the Women's Institute at Watnall, on the outskirts of Nottingham, gave themselves a pat on the back yesterday and they looked decidedly pleased with themselves.

After all, the mild-mannered matrons of Britain's largest women's organization found themselves on the front page of every national newspaper for humiliating the prime minister.

The WI is described as a charity, does not describe itself as a political organization, seeing itself more as a modern voice for women.

Downing Street was yesterday privately angry at such a claim, pointing out that the WI repeatedly lobbies government and openly espouses its views in clear political terms.

Ministers do not want to engage in an open war of words with the WI, partly because there are few political benefits from doing so, but one minister said: 'We are lobbied up to 30 times a year. They produce papers on how to lobby MPs and MEPS, how to deal with lobbying organizations, how parliament works and it even in the past adopted a position on the future of the lords.'

The map gap can be seen between the prime minister's office and representatives of the Women's Institute. The prime minister attended a large WI conference and offered his view of a vision of Britain. For the delegates at the event this was a blatant political campaign message and not what they expected to hear. As a result he was booed, hissed at and received a slow hand-clap.

The map gap here can be seen in the way people perceive what the WI stands for. They view themselves as a 'modern voice for women'. But the map being use by the government is that it 'lobbies government and espouses its views in clear political terms'. Neither side disagrees that the event took place, but the gap has emerged over a clear understanding of the status of the group. As long as this map gap exists it will block any headway that might be made to resolve the conflict. Unfortunately, to overcome any conflict of this type, both sides have to reach a position where they have a shared map of events.

Map versus territory

Any map we hold in our head is representation of the territory. It can never be the real thing because it isn't the real thing. If you want to know what it feels like to walk across the Sahara desert, then you have to do it. Reading a book on North Africa just won't give you access to that experience.

What we see in our heads isn't what exists.

Unfortunately, people believe that their internal representation *is* the territory. They believe that their understanding is the truth and that no other variation can exist. Take a look at any form of extremism. Apartheid, fascism, religious cults, even football hooliganism, are based on the premise that theirs is the only answer (or football team). Where such dogma exists it becomes difficult to build bridges and develop any sense of shared success.

Exposing the person to the facts, as they exist and as perceived by other people, is one way of achieving this. My insistence that I was giving the right directions to Bourne End was only pulled short when Lin found out that actually there are two Bourne Ends. Now I could have disagreed with that, but in reality once she pointed it out then I could understand the problem. We sometimes have to go through this process to help people with entrenched beliefs step inside out, for a while and see the world from a different perspective.

Positive thinking

No matter how much I cajoled, encouraged, supported and motivated (shouted at!) Lin, it didn't help her to discover that she was in the wrong county! This is one of the dangers with the positive-thinking ethos. While it's good to take a positive view of your situation, if you're deep in the mire to start with, you'll need to step back a bit and find a new perspective.

Consider the companies that have nearly folded over recent years. Saying 'Now, just be a bit more positive' to IBM when they hit problems might have earned the consultants some money, but would it really have made a great deal of difference? They had to step back and reframe who they were and their position in the market.

From a personal perspective, when the company I worked for started their downsizing program, I felt really low, couldn't understand what to do, and retreated into my shell. The reality was that the company's cost base was increasing and their income was falling. Positive talk and thoughts don't do great deal of good in this situation. The company had a choice: increase revenues, or cut costs. Although it embarked on the generation of new revenue streams, this takes time and that was a luxury the company didn't have. So, we had to cut costs, and one of the biggest costs in most companies is people.

I needed to take action. The moment I stopped trying to think positive and started to enhance my personal variety, life changed almost overnight. By stepping back and looking at what else I might do to resolve my problem, I could see with greater clarity what was going on. I started to understand the maps being used by the senior managers to drive their decisions. I tried to understand the maps being used by my colleagues and how their restricted variety limited personal choice. Most importantly, I tried to understand the maps being used in the markets where I might be able to get a job. By adopting a broader view I was able to make choices that got me out of the situation.

The acceptable truth

Making a shift in our personal maps requires accepting another person's truth. There's often a tendency for the inner voice to chirp away in the background offering a running commentary on the world. As we watch news broadcasts, read the paper or listen to people talk, a switch toggles between 'I agree' and 'I disagree.' We do this without even realizing what the inner voice is doing, but it can have a powerful impact on how we act and respond in different situations. Just reading this paragraph, your inner voice will have said 'yes, that's right,' or prompted you to feel irritated at the fact that someone else asserted that you don't have logical control over how you behave.

Unacceptable ◄————————————————► Acceptable

Figure 28 *Acceptability line*

The difference between what you find acceptable and unacceptable can be quite straightforward like 'I don't like the taste of whisky', or it might be a more subtle preference where you happen to prefer a certain type of whisky. It might be difficult to separate acceptable from unacceptable where the separation is unclear, and, of course, preferences can change from day to day, but it's important to have some understanding of where your preferences lie on the acceptability line (Figure 28) and what they mean to you, because ultimately this delineation drives the choices you make.

UA maps

One of the important aspects of the 'map your map' choice and the head dimension is to understand and map some of your unacceptable and acceptable (UA) preferences (see Figure 29). Just think about it. To what extent do you know what you know? How

I find this ...

Unacceptable	Acceptable

Figure 29 *My unacceptable/acceptable (UA) preferences*

successfully could you sit down and describe 'you' to someone else in terms of preferences? I'm sure you could gleefully list your partner's, friends' or boss's UA preferences, but when it comes to your own it can be quite difficult. Why not give it a try? Don't just go for the obvious ones, try to look at some of the deeper aspects that really drive how you think, feel and behave. For example, how do you feel about eating meat, fox hunting, children who scream in restaurants, dog lovers who don't scoop the poop, kids who get drunk in your town on a Friday night, or the use of chlorine in the water system? Try to think of the many judgements your inner voice makes.

When I had to hit the deadline for this book, I decided to go away on my own for a week and leave the trials and tribulations of family life behind me. I called into the travel agents and booked the first cheap holiday that I could get that was guaranteed to get me some sun. While writing this section, I just stopped for a while and watched life go on around me, but I also listened to my inner voice rattling away as it offered comments on the passing world. It was an enlightening and powerful experience. In the space of ten minutes my inner voice passed comments on:

◆ hotels that leave open bottles of vodka next to the children's bowl of orange

◆ children allowed to run by the pool where it's slippery

◆ the check-out time for the last day

- being in an all-English hotel
- women sunbathing topless
- Minorca in comparison to Malta
- the wisdom of eating meat.

Now for all of these fleeting thoughts, there was ultimately a UA decision being made and filed away as a frame of reference for the future. While I'm conscious of these processes and UA allocation, I can step back and challenge the inner voice forming the inner maps. This is part of the rationale for building your UA map. Just by writing from the heart, rather than from the head, you can start to understand how you frame life, what causes you to make decisions, and which of your UA preferences you're happiest with. By mapping how you map, you can start to choose how you might like your map to look.

While you're mapping your map, it might be useful to understand how other people map their UA preferences (see Figure 30). Just what do other people find acceptable and unacceptable? Why? And how do their UA maps differ from yours? Think of one person you find it difficult to get along with. Picture them clearly in your mind and start to think about how they think, feel and behave. Try to write down what their UA map looks like.

Consider how much your map differs from theirs. If you can find things that are significantly different, try to think about the gap.

They find this ...

Unacceptable	Acceptable

Figure 30 *Other people's UA preferences*

What is it that's different? If the head map indicates that you are opposites, what in the heart is driving this? Do you have opposite values in life or do you share any likes and dislikes?

Comparative mapping can help you understand the differences between you and the important people in your life.

Take five minutes to draw a UA map for someone you get along with really well (see Figure 31).

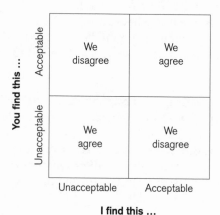

Figure 31 *UA map*

You'll find that with the people you like *and* those you don't like, your maps will never agree. We all have our own maps, they're all different, and none of them is the 'right' one.

Use the UA map to:

◆ understand your UA preferences

◆ choose those you wish to keep

◆ choose those you'll change and choose what the change will be

◆ understand other people's UA maps and accept that they are just that, maps, not truths

◆ start to understand how to build bridges and work in a more effective way with other people.

To lead yourself and others effectively, you must disregard observed behaviour and, instead, start to understand what maps are being used to drive behaviour. If you meet someone you perceive to be offish and withdrawn, ignore that and start to understand what it is that drives that behaviour. You might also start to question where your judgement of their behaviour comes from. I don't know anyone who says they're stand-offish and withdrawn, but I do know lots of people who like to have private space and prefer to get closer to people over a longer timeframe than others. Rather than them being distant, it might be that you have certain drivers in your unacceptable frame that cause you to be against such behaviour.

UA patterns
The UA map can help us further to develop understanding of conversation and behaviour. It highlights the following:

◆ the boring band

◆ the possibility band

◆ loop mapping

The boring band is so called because there's a good chance that two people operating from these maps will tend to rehash old ideas and discussions rather than being generative in their approach. Consider Figure 32, where you have groups of people who share similar maps on what is acceptable and unacceptable. There is a chance they will simply agree on everything and agree to disagree on things they don't agree on. This is not to suggest that people who share similar UA maps will never be creative, but any creativity is likely to be bounded within the maps that already exist.

Contrasting the pattern in Figure 33, with the possibility band there is a good chance that sparks will fly and new ideas will be created from the fusion of these minds. People with different UA maps will walk into areas they might have deemed wrong in relation to their personal domain. The power of possibility within this band comes, not necessarily from the heat of the disagreement, but more when they know and accept that they have different maps, and that that's precisely why they've come together.

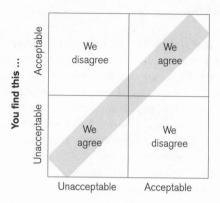

Figure 32 *The boring band*

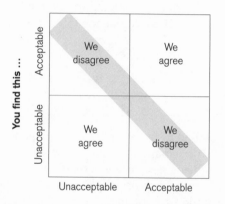

Figure 33 *The possibility band*

For example, if sales of a product are falling, the response from people operating in the boring band might be to alter the promotional discount, increase the number of outlets, or in extreme cases fire the product manager. For people in the possibility band, they will adopt a more generative approach and challenge each other to think on some of the broader problems. They might ask richer questions about the falling sales of a product. To what extent is there conflict in the market place with other products the company sells? Are cross-portfolio problems emerging? Has research and development lagged so that the product has become dated? Are the sales performance targets at odds with the needs of the product turnover levels?

The key to the possibility band is in the art of turning the questions back on themselves through the use of shared dissonance to create new options and possibilities. They would ask what underlying assumptions are being made, and what are the values of the questioner in suggesting that a problem exists in the first place. For example, instead of a manager trying to determine why the performance of a team member has fallen, they might ask themselves why it took so long to notice, or what steps are being taken to develop *all* the individuals in the team.

The possibility band is a place where new and original ideas come to the fore – a metaphor that describes the areas that people can go to, but normally prefer to avoid.[4] Often when exploring new ways of working or thinking, arbitrary and self-imposed constraints exist that prevent people and organizations from tackling normal problems in new and innovative ways. There can be a tendency to stick with the knitting, play safe and stay inside the comfort zone. Even worse is the desire to keep other people in their comfort zone. By fusing people together who don't agree, it's possible to create new shared maps that exceed the breadth and depth of the current ones.

The final pattern is loop mapping, where energy and ideas are wasted because a group of people, all with different maps, compete against each other rather than creating new options.

In a team environment, if you get to a point where map blockage has occurred, it helps to set a rolling pattern within the team (see Figure 34). Starting in the 'We agree' box, find something that you all agree on. Once the team is at ease, move to the 'Let's disagree' box, where you have the chance to present your own views and ideas on what's right and see how they differ from other people's. Give the team the freedom to critique your assumptions and help realign your map. Move on to 'Let's agree what we don't find acceptable' to define the

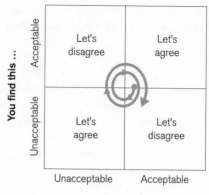

Figure 34 *Loop mapping*

outer boundary of the group, and, finally, go on to what *you* find unacceptable, and others are happy with. Try to understand why the difference is there and how it might be used to create new options.

Keep following this loop pattern until you're able to accept the other people's maps and hopefully have stretched the total map of the group to new levels. Loop mapping is hugely beneficial because it avoids the traditional confrontation and battle-based approach to group working and introduces a sweeping style that is inclusive but still challenging and dynamic. The underlying dynamic is a give–get orientation. At one point you might be giving your UA map to others, and then five minutes later you're in an inquiry state, trying to get from them how they view the world. The energy and synthesis of this interaction creates a new generative model of group working that is stretching but safe.

Fantasy league

Our mental maps are not rigid but this means they can become distorted over time and what appears to be the truth or a correct decision one day might appear totally different on another day. This distortion can be almost imperceptible and is driven by many factors, including personal values, political forces, fears or simple forgetfulness. The shift from hard, objective data to subjective fiction can quite rapidly take you through a number of stages (see Figure 35), based on the Ladder of Inference developed by Chris Argyris:

1 I see something happen that is quite factual.

2 I select details from what I observe, based on my beliefs and values.

3 I use these details and add my personal meanings, based on personal experiences.

4 This view shifts from interpretation to hard fact.

5 I take actions and change my behaviour, based on these new beliefs.

At the bottom of the ladder is a fact or event that happens to you. You select elements of the event and turn it into *faction*, something that is basically true but is influenced and modified by our map of the world. The faction turns into fiction, as the biased story is translated into a distorted view of what happened – although some element of the fact can be found, you would have to dig quite deep to uncover the real events. Finally, the fiction turns into fantasy as the story takes on mythical status. This may be triggered by the original fact, but has nothing to do with it in terms of either content or detail.

This happens all the time in the political arena. A new and reputable politician gets elected to Parliament. They build a reputation as a good politician and an honest broker. But in a television interview

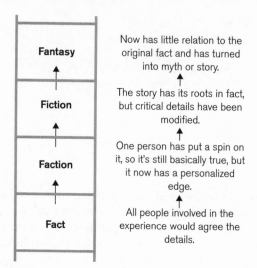

Figure 35 *Fantasy league*

they make a comment that seems to contradict statements made in an earlier campaign. People start to mistrust the politician and this links readily with the stereotypical view of politicians who make promises and break them. The politician is branded a liar and manipulator and further tales get them deselected at the earliest opportunity. What was a slight shift in political position becomes a radical turn around in political posture.

Personal fantasy league
The climb up the fantasy league doesn't have to involve other people. This is something that you do individually, and often in seconds. Think about the last time you made a presentation to an audience. All's going well until you realize that the man at the end of the third row is not paying attention. The closer you look you realize that he is actually typing away on his laptop. Immediately, the insecurity driver kicks in, and you think that your presentation is failing. You start to climb up to the faction level as you conclude that other people are probably not interested either and are just looking interested to be polite. Then you reach the fiction stage where you believe that your presentational style is all wrong. You're not clever enough, you look like a mess and don't have any funny stories to draw upon like the really good presenters. By the end, you've made a headlong jump into fantasy and decided that you'll never do any more of this type of presentation – you're not up to it and it's far better coming from someone who knows what they're doing.

This leap up the ladder is a common event and one that people beat themselves up over on a daily basis. If not during a presentation then it might be how you react in a team meeting, at a family gathering, or at college. The point is that we often climb the league without any real need to. We let the insecurity and restricted variety drivers build conclusions about us and others that are unclear or totally false. In the case of the presentation, it might have been that the man at the end of the row was really enthused about your presentation and wanted to capture all the elements that weren't in the overheads.

Unless you take time to climb down the league and operate at fact level, you'll be forever operating in fantasy land.

Shared fantasy league

Imagine you've had an argument with someone at work. Although it's a silly spat that you manage to resolve, you can see how it starts to make its way up the fantasy ladder. At the time both you and the other person might be able to describe what happened, and your descriptions would match closely enough. But just moments after it happens, you call a close colleague and describe the argument to them. You put small, personal spins on the situation so, at the second level, your description is still true, but your personal embellishments have turned it into faction. Your friend will meet others at work and tell them what happened, but this time they put their own spin on the situation. At this point the story takes a leap from faction to fiction. The event being described, though recognizable, is now different. Your friend wants to enhance your position and the story is increasingly focused on what you did right and what the other person did wrong. So much of the truth has been replaced with distorted information. And, finally, the word gets spread about what happened and the tale takes on enormous changes as more and more personal views are added in.

The original event becomes a fantasy that has very little to do with fact.

But remember, *both* sides of the story have climbed the fantasy ladder and we can see how a gap or canyon can emerge in the relationship (see Figure 36).

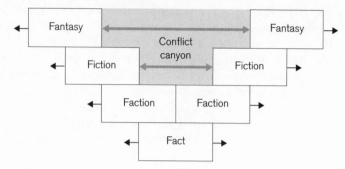

Figure 36 *Fantasy canyon*

Fantasy provides the potential for conflict. The escalation from fact to fantasy leads to conflict at home, at work, on the sports field, and even to wars between nations. Take any major conflict and it's generally possible to trace back each side's story to a root fact or incident. The irony is that once the fantasy is built on each side, the conflict is no longer about anything substantial – it's simply about egos, beliefs, political position and power.

Some fissures are only small and the fantasy gap can be resolved by climbing down the league and re-agreeing the real facts. However, a fissure can split so far that the conflict starts to cause a real problem. And, once the fantasy story is public and in place, it can be hard for both sides to climb down the ladder to talk about the real rather than the fictitious issue.

Fantasy forces

This type of reframing can be seen in the home as we make distinctions between right and wrong based on our relationships with other family members. When I was a teenager and lived with my parents, the house we lived in wasn't a big place and, as the lounge was small, we didn't have a lot of space. When the dinner table was set up, it used to be quite difficult to find a free space to put your tea cup or soft drink. One day I walked into the lounge and didn't see the coffee cup that my mother had put down on the floor next to her chair. Within a second the coffee was all over the carpet and we were rushing around trying to get a cloth to mop it up before the coffee stained. At the time my dad chewed me out for being careless and not looking where I was going. Fair enough, I thought, he was right, it was my fault. The next day, as I crashed out to watch the wrestling on a Saturday afternoon, I put the cup on the floor next to my chair. In walked my mother who promptly sent the cup flying, and yet again we scrabbled to find a cloth to mop the tea up before it stained the carpet. Now dad chewed me out for putting the cup on the floor. I couldn't believe it! I tried to tell him how unfair he was being, but to no avail, he was in full flow and nothing was going to stop him.

I believe that my dad's natural intuition to defend mum led him to form decisions in each instance as to what had happened and who was to blame. In both cases he passionately believed that he was right. This is because he was influenced by the legacy of his relationships with us all (mine was that I was a slob and left rubbish all over the place) and his personal values and beliefs (see Figure 37). These were driven by his love of my mother and a natural desire to support her. She had the job of running the household and none of us were great at helping her. So although the facts were broadly the same, he formed a rapid interpretation based on what he believed and what had happened in the past.

The question is, to what extent do *you* do the same? If you have a problem with a team member or co-worker, do you try to stay at the fact level and deal with the problem based upon what happens? Or do you build on your past relationship with your colleague and race up the ladder, and end up trying to resolve a fantasy problem?

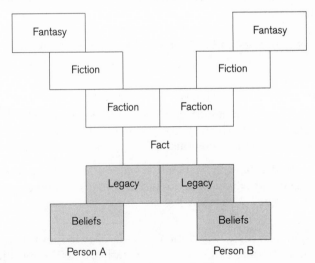

Figure 37 *The foundations of the shared fantasy ladder*

From fantasy to fact

Ultimately, the only way down conflict canyon is through the use of productive conversations. These are conversations that help tackle underlying issues that sit beneath the words we use when talking. The first point is to agree that there is a difference of viewpoint. Once this is agreed, we have a safe way to stop the fissure in its tracks and we can ask several questions:

- What are the observable facts that drive the statements being made?

- Do we both agree on the facts as offered?

- Can you run me through your viewpoint and why you believe certain things?

- How did we get from those facts to the current situation?

- What difference do you see between my view of the situation and yours?

- Will you let me try and understand why you feel this way about the issue?

- What is important to you personally?

These questions are used to specifically climb down the ladder and drop below fact level, to understand the person, more than just the situation.

As you try to understand the deeper issues, there are two areas to consider:

- What are the legacy choices that you and the other person have made in the past that impact on the issue? What is your history together and is this history a factor that will prevent you from having a productive relationship?

- Do you understand the beliefs and values that are important to the person and which have an impact on the creation of any fantasy league?

In the majority of cases, the climb up the fantasy ladder is driven by deep-rooted personal values and beliefs rather than the specifics of the circumstances. Only when the legacy and values are understood

can you stand any chance of moving down the fantasy league to deal
with the fact of the problem.

The football manager who constantly argues with one of the star players is actually fighting a beliefs battle, where he believes that the manager has to operate a firm command and control regime, whereas the footballer believes that the effective sportsperson has to be free in order to release their talent.

Admittedly, this type of productive conversation is rarely easy. Even the simplest question about how someone else views their world can feel like a challenge to their beliefs. If you really want to step down and operate at fact level, one approach is to operate from a position of disclosure first, inquiry second and advocacy third. In this way, once you display that you're prepared to share your framework, then understand another person's world view, it becomes easier to understand how their frame might not fit with the leadership frame you're trying to install.

Professional map-makers
The problem with the fantasy league is that maps can be based on 'facts' which are actually fantasy. Every day tabloid myths are perpetuated because people believe what they read. On a grander scale a whole nation can turn fact into fantasy. A child reared in an environment where, for example, racial discrimination is accepted, or even favoured, might know deep down that lies and falsehoods have been spun in order to ensure a certain form of political power is maintained. And the titans of corporate concerns, media moguls and political parties employ large teams just to manage people's maps. If you take one step back and map your map of the world, how much of it is built on fact, and how much is based on fantasy? And how do you know the difference between the two?

Who mapped your map?
What filters and tests can you apply to ensure you're not being fed information that's clouded with fictional additions by those who have played with the ideas. For example, how do you know if the latest

story from your chairperson is fact, faction, fiction or fantasy? To what extent are you confident that the feedback you received at your last appraisal wasn't clouded?

It's the transfer of one person's fantasy to another's fact that leads to grapevine growth in organizations (see Figure 38).

Person A is at a meeting where the director briefs the team about a new pay scheme that will be due next year. But they push it up the league and believe that the new pay scheme is actually designed to cut the overall pay budget. Person A tells B, B turns it into a belief that the pay budget must be cut because the business is in trouble, and in effect, they now believe that the company has major financial

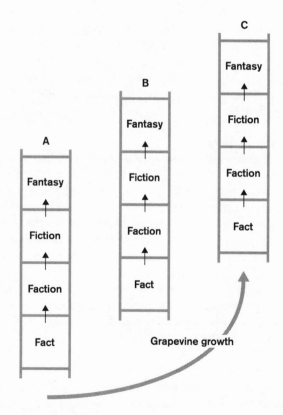

Figure 38 *Grapevine growth*

problems and might be looking to make people redundant. B tells C this story and C infers a new fantasy that job cuts are imminent. All these people are receiving other people's fantasies and have little appreciation of the real facts of the matter.

Think about the headings below. Consider how you would describe your beliefs on each one:

◆ the political situation in this country

◆ the current economic situation

◆ the extent to which religious integration should be encouraged

◆ the extent to which gay sex should be more openly discussed.

Once you've considered your views on each of these topics, ask yourself:

◆ Do I trust my information sources not to have pushed the details up the fantasy ladder?

◆ Do I trust their sources not to have pushed the information up the league?

◆ Do I make time to read opposing views to counter-balance the current map and test where my views are on the league?

◆ Am I confident that my current map of the world is unbiased and free of fantasy contamination?

If you can answer yes to these questions, your map is no doubt pristine, accurate and unbounded – congratulations! But be careful. You may have developed the ability to see the world as it is and acquire rich variety in the way you view life, but I'm sure that most racist and bigoted political parties have such a view. It's far better to believe that your view is biased and corrupted, then you'll always seek to test and validate your map of the world, rather than sitting back on the assumption that you've got it right.

Throughout the process of mapping your map you should create opportunities wherever you can to enrich your variety, and avoid accepting other people's views of the world. If you choose not to review your map and to stick with your current version, you've locked yourself into a kind of self-imprisonment. This can only ever limit your opportunity to lead yourself and others in a more effective way. Your map has to be flexible.

If you see beauty in art and I see paint then I lose.

If you see the sunrise in the morning and I hear the dogs barking, then I lose. If you see market opportunities and I see market problems, then I lose. We all have the freedom to see the world as we wish to see it or as others see it. The important thing is to choose the choice and not fritter it away through apprehension or apathy.

Map expansion

One way to enrich your variety is to seek out, map and explore other people's maps. As the two views contrast, conflict and coalesce, you can create a new view of the world that is unique and full of possibilities. Only by appreciating how people who work with you see their experiences can you hope to share sustainable and profitable relationships with them.

One way to do this is by using the framework shown in Figure 39. There are a number of ways to look at the world, but in essence they all boil down to 'my view' and 'your view', where the 'you' includes everyone else apart from 'me'. At the moment there are maps that I have of the world that make sense and there are things in the world that I can't see. The map inquiry matrix suggests that I might undertake two journeys of discovery.

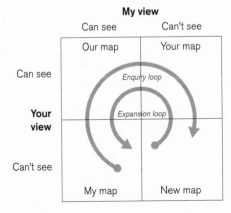

Figure 39 *Map inquiry*

The first is to start from a view of the world that is essentially my map. This is a view that I have but which you don't see.

I then start on an inquiry journey to understand how you view the world that we both operate in. At this point I am in the 'our map' segment. From there I can inquire how you look at life in areas that I've never experienced. At this stage we both understand the world we share and the world outside of our boundaries. We have created a new map for ourselves, one that has more variety than when we started.

Once we understand the differences between our two maps, we can start the expansion journey. I can start to pull your experiences, values and maps into my view of the world. I can try to understand the points of view that differ from mine and then assimilate them into my frame of reference. At the end of the journey I've arrived back at the 'my map' quadrant, though now I have a broader, richer and deeper understanding of how you see the world and therefore richer variety within my own map.

As the revised map inquiry matrix in Figure 40 shows, at the end of the expansion and assimilation process we have both increased the size of 'our map' so the 'our map' quadrant has now increased in size, ideally by more than a factor of two. The process of inquiry and assimilation should not be a doubling process. If effective, it will prove to be a compound exercise where the synergies that arise from our shared map introduce concepts and ideas that we've never

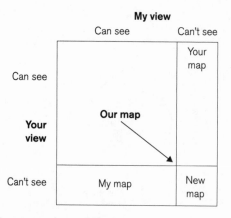

Figure 40 *Map inquiry: our map expanded*

encountered before. The shape and size of the new map quadrant in this matrix is quite deliberate and suggests that there is probably a finite limit to the extent to which you can expand your map by working through the expansion process with one person. The objective is to repeat this exercise with as many people as possible in order to increase and expand the variety of your world view.

Breaking free from your own perspective and drawing maps that have been influenced by others will leave you better equipped to understand and manage the complex everyday world of organizations and relationships.[5]

Map your map: quick summary

◆ Your mental maps are the lenses through which you see and make sense of the world. They are unique to you and are an essential part of who you are and how you lead. If your maps are corrupted they constrain and negate your ability to lead others and yourself.

◆ To learn to help others learn you must be able to break up your old maps and create new and more informed views. By breaking and making maps, you effect changes in the way you behave.

◆ Your map of the world is not *the* world; it's a representation of what you choose to observe through biased and subjective lenses. Never accept what you observe as the truth.

◆ Positive thinking can help you develop your abilities, but it will be of little use if you're using an out-of-date or inappropriate map of the world.

◆ As you reframe messages to fit your maps, don't shift them up the fantasy ladder. By moving an event from fact to fantasy, you're deceiving yourself and, even worse, you might deceive someone else if you pass such a message on.

◆ Conflict is caused because your map is different to another's and both of you argue that yours is 'right'.

◆ Combining your map with someone else's will create a third map that is richer in variety and experience than the two single maps you started with.

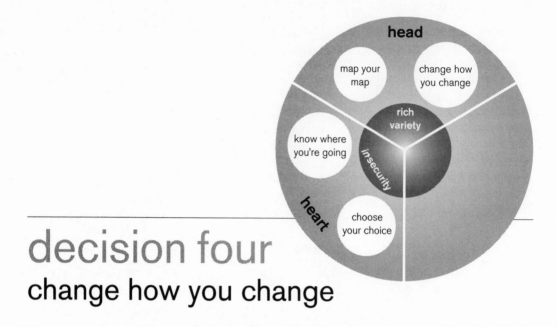

decision four
change how you change

It is only the wisest and the very stupidest who cannot change.

Confucius

From producing two albums in a Newcastle bedsit to being short-listed for the Mercury prize for the best album of the year is quite a significant achievement. Kathryn Williams cut her first album for £80 on her bedsit label and then spent £200 to enter the Mercury prize. The big labels were soon knocking at her door and A&R men were ringing her at home to persuade her to join them. But she's happy where she has control over her music. She likes doing what she is doing the way she does it.[6] She didn't care that she might not win the prize because she had broken through the barrier that prevents so many musicians attracting the interest of the market.

The power of this message is that Kathryn hasn't followed the normal path to gain access to the market. She realized she had a choice and that choice was to spend £200 on the entry fee in preference over taxing her car. As a result she bypassed much of the tortuous, drawn out route that so many artists follow to gain the attention of the music industry. There are two guiding factors that helped her along this journey. The first is a clear understanding of the purpose and outcome that she wanted to achieve. The second is the ability to adopt a change style that was different from that of her peers and the industry.

Essentially she seemed to be unafraid of the process of change. In developing such leadership capability a sense of change mastery can be achieved, and with this comes a new type of comfort and protection. Rather than being a threatening and disrupting process, Rosabeth Moss Kanter suggests that change can be regarded as a new form of security. In the more traditional organization, security is based on the acquisition of power: the power to hold resources, discipline people, control finances and build personal empires. In organizations that value knowledge, people's ability to synthesize the energy of change and learning ultimately offers a greater degree of influence and control than the ability to accumulate hierarchical power, and therefore change offers greater security.

Two primary change ideas are considered in this decision:

♦ **The change ladder.** Change is a holistic process that transforms the tangible to intangible elements. It can't be separated into discrete levels.

♦ **Change style.** The process of change can be managed using four styles that vary in structure and visibility.

The change ladder

Changing how we change is at the heart of any personal leadership process so that we can respond to shifts in the market. Such shifts come in various forms: a new management style, the even newer baby in my arms, or a change in eating habits because yet another disease has been found in a particular food product. On a daily basis, personal change means that we have to radically and rapidly make a shift in how we think, feel and behave.

Change fails – but it doesn't have to!

One of the world's biggest industries – the diet industry – is based around this need for people to make quite dramatic shifts in how they respond to the demands placed on them by themselves or others. Everywhere I go people are in one of three phases, about to diet (pre-new year's day), dieting (new year's day), or just finished a diet (new year's day evening). Dieting is a massive preoccupation with a large percentage of the population, and fortunately for the slimming clubs, diet magazines, and food manufacturers, one where people fail to achieve their goal on a regular basis. The industry is huge for the very reason that people fail to 'change how they change'!

And failure to change how we change and deliver long-term sustainable results is not just an individual phenomenon. We see it everywhere we look in the corporate world.

Failure of corporate mergers and acquisitions, Business Process Re-engineering or IT solutions to deliver sustainable results. As Peter Senge says, most change initiatives fail.[7] In many cases the supposed failure rate for total quality and re-engineering initiatives is around the 70 per cent mark. In a study of 100 top management-driven corporate transformation efforts, Harvard's John Kotter concluded that more than half did not survive the initial phase.

Beyond the actual failure to change, companies fail to recognize that they have failed, either because of corporate political intrigue, or because the speed of change disguises the failure. To ensure effective corporate change, companies need to understand more about the soft processes that drive and support change. These are the actions that need to be understood (irrespective of the nature of the change or the industry). However, these 'fuzzy factors' are the intangible elements that get left aside once the change is underway and results are expected by the senior team.

Going back to the idea of the personal change and managing a diet, it's easy to change the type of food you buy, put more structure into how you eat, and learn about new ways of cooking. The problem lies in the intangible area – that little piece of you where you have to make a decision and stick to it. All these other things are external crutches that simply reinforce the fact that you're on a diet – they pale into insignificance against the need to understand at a deep level why you want to lose weight. The same is true of corporate change. All the projects, programmes, models, tools and systems are a waste of time unless the company truly understands why it wants to change and has a deep personal commitment to changing its whole existence or purpose.

The five levels of change
Because of the complexity of deep-level change either on a personal or corporate level, I've devised a framework, called the change ladder (see Figure 41), which allows you to categorize different actions in five distinct groupings. This is a simple but highly effective tool that will help you to understand the holistic nature of personal and business transformation.

Break down change and look at it from the following perspectives:

◆ **Assets** – the tools, plant or equipment used to deliver a product or service. For the company this is land, building and production equipment; for the dieter, this is a change in the food being eaten.

Figure 41 *The change ladder*

- ◆ **Blueprints** – the methods by which you manage how you do things. For the large organization this means the strategic and tactical plans, processes, quality systems and personnel procedures; for the new dot.com company they are the standard internal procedures, IT protocols and the external financial regulations that control the trading operations; for someone on a diet, it means a change in the routines and rules that drive the eating habits.

- ◆ **Capabilities** – the ways and means by which an output is delivered. For an organization they are contained in its people's skills and competencies and its relationship with customers and suppliers; for a golfer it's their ability to outperform competitors on the fairway and to manage the associated PR activities; for a dieter, it means they decide to learn how to cook food without fat of any kind.

- ◆ **Desires** – the deep-seated motivation that drives people to take action. Within an organization this is the reason why people come to work and do what they do. For some, the motivation might be money, for others, a chance to socialize or to pay for their retirement. For the neighbourhood watch organization, it's the need for people to fight burglary; for the dieter, it's the desire to fit in, to look like others or like someone from the cover of a glossy magazine.

◆ **Existence** – the core reason why a person, team or organization exists. For the organization it's the real (as opposed to the stated) values and purpose; at an international level it's the reason why countries will go to war to maintain their national freedom; at a micro level, it's the decision about what charity to give to or how to allocate their time; for our dieter, it's a clear understanding of the reason for the diet and, more importantly, who they are and where they are heading.

Now we can take the change ladder and consider it in a real situation. You're on a diet, so let's look at some of the options you have:

◆ change your level of food intake

◆ change the type of food you eat

◆ eat at different times

◆ train in nutrition

◆ attend a motivational team session

◆ modify your social habits and avoid restaurants

◆ listen to motivational tapes

◆ read books on how to diet

◆ put notices on the fridge

◆ change your shopping habits

◆ keep yourself mentally psyched up

◆ learn how to cook in new ways

◆ take pills to reduce the hunger pains.

All these activities can be seen in the various diet packages offered by clubs and dieticians. We can take these actions and place them within the change ladder framework and see how the overall diet package looks.

| **Existence** | |
| The sense of purpose | No change options |

Desires	
Motivation to change	Attend a motivational team session
	Listen to motivational tapes
	Put notices on the fridge
	Keep yourself mentally psyched up

Capabilities	
Skills and ability	Train in nutrition
	Read books on how to diet
	Learn how to cook in new ways

Blueprints	
How we operate	Eat at different times
	Modify social habits and avoid restaurants
	Change your shopping habits

Assets	
Tangible things	Change level of food intake
	Change the type of food eaten
	Take pills to reduce the hunger pains

The vast majority of the change processes advocated for diets operate on the lower four rungs of the ladder. Now, I'm not suggesting they won't help with the process, but I do believe that much of the time spent on these activities will yield little long-term value unless they are aligned with a real sense of purpose or ethos.

If you go on a diet, you have to be painfully truthful and ask yourself why you're doing it. Is it for you? Is it for your partner? Is it to get promotion? Or is it because that's what all the magazines say that you should do? All of these are desire-level changes that will fail unless held in place at the existence level. Unless you have an absolute belief in why you're attempting this change and how you'll change as a person, whether it be emotionally or spiritually, then all your efforts will fail.

The curse of the new year's resolution
Think of anyone you know who's trying to change something significant in their lives. It might be giving up smoking or drinking, eating meat, sugar or fat, or spending too much time at work. I guarantee that they surround themselves in a protective cloak of action from the first four levels on the change ladder. They talk about how much they want to do it, have learnt new ways of thinking and

behaving, put in place a change program and even thrown out all the sugar in the house. But this will only sustain the change for so long because unless they've truly changed who they are and how they want to exist then their old habits will pull them back to their old ways of thinking, feeling and behaving.

For the company that wants to shift from operating as a bricks and mortar company and move into Internet trading, it isn't just a case of asking a marketing agency to build them a new brand. It means a fundamental re-appraisal of who and what they are, from the top to the bottom. As a manager wanting to change your style of leadership, attending the latest course on leadership techniques will not make it happen. You need to look inside and truly think about what your new person will be like and make an internal shift before you attempt to achieve a change in behaviour.

The problem with this way of thinking is that people will always say I did X or Y and it fixed the problem. With all the changes at the A, B, C and D levels, change can be delivered and will look really effective and locked in. But without a real shift at the E level, reversion will always take place. At some point in the future the old you will return, either with a bang when your resolution to give up drink is blown at the office party, or over a period of time as you convince yourself that one glass at the weekend won't hurt and that leads to one glass of wine a night and then back to the bottle of wine a night.

One of the problems with managing how we change ourselves or others is in the way that we measure the shift in performance. Again, think about how we measure success on a diet. Usually we get on the scales or check to see if an old dress or pair of pants will fit again. But all we are doing here is trying to measure at the asset level. This measures the weight that's gone, it doesn't measure whether we have the sense of purpose not to regain it. We move on to the capability and desire levels, and each measure looks good for that moment in time, but it doesn't measure sustainability.

You must learn how to measure at the E level.

However, effecting change at this level is hard, primarily because it's invisible and subjective (see Figure 42). I can't tell you the extent to which you've changed your sense of purpose about something. Only

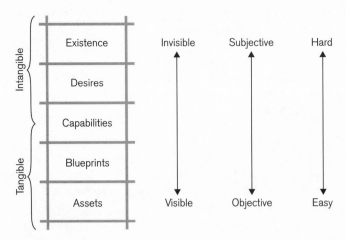

Figure 42 *Change ladder measurement*

you can do this by looking deep inside and being honest with yourself about the level to which you have really changed who you are and where you're going.

The whole purpose of the change ladder is to help you think about how you change from one style of personal leadership to another, to question what changes you need to make and to what extent you're truly prepared to make the deep transformation. If at the end of this book you come up with the solution for your time-management problem: 'That's it! I'll use a new diary system and become a better leader,' don't kid yourself.

Too many people have been on wonderful time-management courses and within a few months revert to a pen and scrappy piece of paper in the top pocket.

Climb the ladder for sustainable change

If you really want to make a change in how you lead yourself then the first thing to do is to mentally climb the top of the ladder and think how the new person will be different. What deep change will there be? Once you understand what will be different, ask yourself if you have the courage to make that type or level of change. If not, then maybe it's best not to attempt it right now. Spend more time thinking about what the new you will be and what trade-offs you're prepared to make to achieve that outcome. If you're prepared to make the transition, put the required changes in at level A, B, C and D to help you on your journey. But remember – it's failure to make a deep and personal change in the E level that leads to new year's resolution syndrome.

Sustainable change for others
Change needs leadership and leadership creates change. It's the process of setting the future and then coaching, guiding, cajoling and helping people to shift to a new way of thinking, feeling and behaving. But if you consider how hard it is to change yourself, you'll understand how difficult it is to change other people.

What is your preferred style of helping others shift to a new way of being? Do you take the asset path and encourage them to change the tangible aspects of their environment? Do you take the blueprint route and help them adopt new processes and procedures? Do you encourage them at the capabilities level to get new skills? Or do you give them a rousing chairman-like speech to change the desire level and kick them off into a new way of operating? Any of these methods are fine but to effect real change you need to spend time on who the individuals are and to what extent they want to be the new person envisaged.

You can't make a person change their E level. That's a private step on the ladder driven by personal choice. Only they can choose their choice and live with the consequences. As any parent who has tried to get their children to keep their bedroom tidy, no matter what techniques, bribery, arguments and inducements are used, if they don't *want* to have a tidy bedroom, it will always revert to the mess they prefer.

Change style

Once you understand the core change you wish to make, think about the style and manner in which you'll manage the transformation. For example, if you want to manage your next career or job shift, will you set things out in detail and plan when your change will be and how it will be managed?

There are four basic styles of change:

◆ **Control.** You follow a planned and visible structure of change, which means making the assumption that you can predict and control your future according to a set of rules. This might be seen in the way we buy a new house or build a garden shed.

◆ **Accidental.** You have a clear understanding of where you want to go, but you don't have a clear process to get there. You're happy to leave events to fate on the basis that the environment is so dynamic that overt control will never work. This might be how you plan a travelling holiday, write a paper at work, decorate the house or design the garden.

◆ **Debate.** Here shift happens through the power of dialogue. You're open about the change and talk to people about the transformation, but don't have a structured approach to how it might be delivered. This might be seen in the way you create a team purpose statement at work or agree the menu for a dinner party.

◆ **Backstage.** You have a clear plan of the way that the change will be managed, but much of the action takes place in corridors or shadow areas. The backstage model is one that we use more than we realize, persuading the children to eat their cabbage; hiding a pill in the dog's food; or flirting with the boss's PA to get some time in his diary.

As you read through the list of styles and descriptors, did you start to disagree with the analogies? For instance, do you feel that the 'right' way to organize a dinner party is through the control method? Or, alternatively, is trying to buy a house through the control method unwise because it's impossible to manage the unmanageable? This reaction indicates that you have a preference for a particular change style.

While your natural and preferred change style might have served you well to date, to survive and prosper in a turbulent world you need to have as broad a range of styles in your personal toolkit as possible.

If your natural style is control, then the accidental approach offers a strong counter-balance, whereas if your natural preference is the backstage fashion, the ability to use debate might soften what is perceived as a political approach to change. The ability and desire to choose how you change can increase your flexibility and ability to operate in a complex and confusing market place.

Change choice

Choosing a change style is determined by the factors that you can influence in the decision-making process. There are two primary choices to be made. First, to what extent will the change be planned? Should every detail be strapped down well in advance of the change commencing or can things be left to chance? Second, how visible will the change be? Is it to be controlled and managed in open view or will it be hidden from sight?

In considering these two drivers, it's possible to identify the four change styles already set out, namely, accidental, backstage, controlled and debate. By looking in more depth at each of these four styles, we can develop a simple change management matrix (see Figure 43). Each of the four quadrants has a particular change style which can be applied in different circumstances.

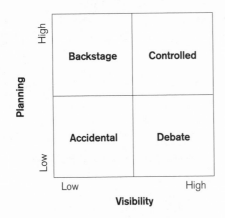

Figure 43 *Change matrix*

Accidental style

When a group of young children play together where there is no formal leader to dictate how they play and interact, their play has an almost chaotic feel. The chance of anything productive coming out of their antics is accidental in nature. However, there are a number of powerful rules that control how the group operates.

The children are effectively operating as a self-organizing system. Although a parent or teacher has set out a number of ground rules, for example, no swearing, no playing on the road, the children are allowed to operate as free agents. Since the parents or teachers are also aware of these rules, they can initiate a change and, within reason, guarantee that a desired outcome is achieved. Just drawing some white lines will trigger games associated with the patterns. And the children understand that when the whistle blows, they are expected to stop and listen for instructions.

Translate this to a work environment. A regional manager in a retail organization has stock wastage higher then the industry norm. She must reduce it to an acceptable level. One option is to issue dictates, discipline people or change the formal stock control procedures. This might seem to work but the ingrained behaviours are likely to surface at a later date once the manager's attention is focused elsewhere. However, by using the accidental methodology, the manager can attempt to understand what rules or norms cause the wastage to happen and why it's seen as acceptable by local managers. It might be that at the store level, wastage costs are attributed to a hidden budget line, visible only to the regional manager and the finance department, so the operational managers are not actually affected by the wastage and it's not part of their frame of reference. By simply changing the bonus indicators, the regional manager might be able to deliver a radical reduction in wastage. The change will have been managed without any real control or planning and its visibility is limited, but the end result is a successful change.

Accidental change is a high-risk strategy and is reliant on the trust of the organization to adopt any changes promoted by the management team.

The manager's role is about helping to develop a suitable environment for the change to occur rather than formalizing any direct approach.

With this style you must love the turbulence. To lead yourself and others effectively you must be able to adapt to the chaotic forces that surround your life. When taking action that is designed to produce a specific outcome, unexpected responses are to be anticipated and actively welcomed. Therefore the key attribute for any individual who seeks to control their life is to be gloriously happy when working with uncertainty.

Backstage style

Remember the millions of people who went to see the film *Titanic*. The boat scenes are truly amazing, to the point where the audience believes they're actually part of the production. Although star actors play a critical front-stage role, it's often the backstage people that can make or break such a film. The power of the backstage processes is apparent.

The key to managing any backstage process is preparation, preparation and more preparation. Just to get a simple scene in a film will take hours and hours of pre-production effort. The installation of a new IT system, the shift to a new quality directive or the adoption of a new legal ruling – all of these will be highly managed and planned but will in the main be invisible to the end user.

The backstage approach requires your exercise of power, persuasion and political skills. It involves intervening in political and cultural systems, influencing, negotiating, selling ideas and meaning[8] to the owners and recipients of the change and mobilizing the necessary power to effect the backstage activity.

Imagine you're going to install a new quality system into a medium-sized manufacturing company. You might choose to operate across a number of backstage areas. The first step is to agree the content of the system with the company directors. Next, you need to negotiate with the key stakeholders to ensure that the content of the system fits with their map of the world. Finally, much of the backstage work will be focused on managing people's feelings. So, although there will be effort applied in developing the new system, a large chunk of the work will be focused on the backstage issues, the unseen aspects that will never be apparent to the end user.

When the backstage approach is overtly used, you must be careful that you're not seen to be using the process in a duplicitous way for personal gain.

In working with a client group, there will always be a degree of suspicion about your actions. When this model is used it's imperative that it's used openly and without any hidden agendas. This doesn't mean that you go round telling everyone what's happening, simply that if people ask about the process being used you take time to explain it.

Controlled style

Controlled change is best used when managing large processes, for example, a large construction project like the Channel Tunnel. The sheer scale and risk means that everything down to the last nut and bolt must be forecast and controlled to ensure that the change is managed to time, cost and quality.

The control model is based on a deterministic framework. This means you assume that it's possible to predict and control the future according to a set of rules. Plans are made, resources booked and people hired on the premise that the change will follow a known path. The change is then managed using the exception method, where the goal is to minimize any variance or disturbance in the system. Accidents will be frowned on, deviation isn't allowed and failure to hit a milestone will cause apoplexy.

This method is perfect for the delivery of fixed outcomes, particularly where the plan is built using logical cause-and-effect reasoning. But, with a rigid plan, all your eggs are definitely in one basket.

Debate style

Think about a merger between two large organizations. Project managers, probably using the control method outlined above, will wrap up all the mechanistic issues. However, there will be elements of the merger that can't be managed using a highly planned style. There is likely to be a large amount of debate and dialogue as people struggle to come to terms with new working cultures. Only though a process of sharing and working together will people start to understand what value their new partners will be able to contribute.

The debate style of change is seen in many areas. In reality, corporate strategy emerges from dialogue and debate that goes on between the key players in the business. This might happen in formal meetings but in many cases it takes place through the odd comment as people meet in corridors or coffee rooms.

The debate model happens all the time but is often not recognized, since it's so natural and embedded in the content of the change. The benefit is that when the change takes place, it's locked in at the desire level in the change ladder, which guarantees a greater degree of passion and permanence.

head

lead yourself

momentum

The emergent style

By drawing on all four styles, you can develop a holistic framework, a hybrid model that builds on the strengths of each but avoids their weaknesses (see Figure 44).

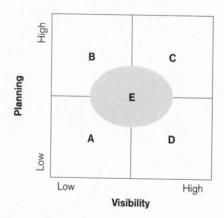

Figure 44 *The emergent change matrix*

If a group of people decide to travel around the world on a back-packing holiday, which of the four styles would be appropriate? The accidental approach is exciting but could leave them sitting as hostages in some war zone. The backstage model would be ineffective because only the travel agent would know the itinerary. The control model seems to be the most practical, but using a deterministic approach in a chaotic world will only lead to frustration and cost increases as the travellers struggle to keep in line with 'the plan'. Finally the debate model is pretty inappropriate since the group might have fun discussing where to go next but the trip will probably take three years longer than expected. Realistically, there is a need to adopt a change process that produces clearly defined outcomes with necessary flexibility.

In considering the five-segment model, each of the four primary models (accidental, backstage, control and debate) has a clear role to play in managing change. Emergent style is practised widely but not knowingly. Your life is often in tension between planned and unplanned events; it's a battle between order and disorder seen in the deletions and changes in your diary. However, your ability to manage unplanned and emergent interactions allows you to respond to changes in the market place. The emergent model gives you the flexibility to adapt and respond to any situation that work or life might throw at you. You have the discipline to tightly manage a problem that has to be delivered within a set timescale; the flexibility to work with a team of people who don't wish to be overtly controlled; the skills to use conversations and dialogue as a way to change how people think and feel; and the shrewdness to operate in the backstage area when a high profile would be detrimental.

Change how you change: quick summary

◆ Leadership results in change and change needs leadership.

◆ The journey to effective leadership will always entail some degree of transformation or change. Therefore you need to have different change maps, alternative routes you can take to achieve the desired outcome. Abdication of the choice to manage change is a failure to lead.

◆ Any change, whether it's personal or corporate is systemic. It's impossible to change one part of the system without impacting on another in some way. Failure to understand the systemic nature of change leads to persistent failure wherever managed change occurs.

◆ The change ladder offers a simple tool to help define the level of change occurring. Each level needs to be addressed to ensure both tangible and intangible aspects of the transition are sustainable.

◆ There are five primary levels within the change ladder: assets, blueprints, capabilities, desires and existence. The areas of the change ladder that are most commonly addressed are assets and blueprints, and desire and existence are most often forgotten. Measurement is easy at the lower levels and becomes more difficult as you climb the ladder, but for change to be effective you must climb the whole way up to ensure that the upper levels are being addressed.

◆ The four change styles are accidental, backstage, control and debate. Accidental change offers freedom and creativity but comes with the risk of non-completion where the outcome is unclear. Backstage change offers huge returns as the political and social systems are managed but it can appear selfish or clandestine. Control change can deliver in mission-critical situations but may limit the spirit and resourcefulness of the people involved. Debate change opens up the change process for all to get involved but can lead to chaos as the people take over – the optimum position is to adopt an emergent style where you have the freedom and flexibility to use any of the four styles at any moment.

hand
leadership in action

Few things can help an individual more than to place responsibility on him, and to let him know that you trust him.

Booker T. Washington

At some stage you'll need to work and collaborate with others to create a shared success. The hand dimension is about how you behave, how you conduct yourself in order to achieve your personal goals; in particular, it relates to how you create effective relationships to help achieve the outcomes you desire. The core driver for the hand function is the ability to develop and maintain trust-based relationships with other people.

Oil the relationship

Trust is the oil that lubricates relationships.

With relationships grounded in trust, the relationship will be open, transferable and often celebrated. Where a relationship is grounded in distrust, power bases and back-biting, success will be token, short-lived and sour. Low-trust relationships are characterized by face-saving, setting out boundaries, and the creation of power positions. Furthermore, this emphasis interferes with and distorts the perceptions of problems, causing them to seem insurmountable, or creating problems that do not exist.[9]

Trust is the fulcrum that can effect different degrees of leverage in a relationship. By shifting the fulcrum towards the high-trust direction, you can quantify the reduction in time taken to solve problems and work effectively. Within an organization the transaction costs reduce if less money is spent on monitoring and control processes. If people don't have to worry about making mistakes and protecting their turf, they're more willing to open up and share learning and knowledge. Correspondingly, as the fulcrum shifts the other way, trust diminishes, power battles erupt, tribal camps form and the flow of knowledge is attenuated.

However, trust isn't a simple switch that can be turned on and off at will. The giving and taking of trust can vary considerably in its fragility and resilience, and can change quickly or slowly depending on the circumstances. Trust associated with a close personal friendship is resilient and durable, and can be regarded as thick trust. Once established, it's not easily disrupted, but once shattered, it isn't readily repaired or restored.[10] In casual or short-term relationships, we see thin trust. This is the type conferred on a project group or product team, where people only tend to commit part of themselves.

Trust funds

It took me a long time to realize that I can't really achieve anything successful in my life without the help of others. To deliver something in life that has value and is sustainable it must be achieved by working in partnership with others, people who have a shared goal and will work towards the same or shared outcome.

How do you build and maintain such productive relationships? What are the critical factors that you put in place both to identify people you can work with and to maintain the relationships over a satisfactory time? They are all centred on the notion of trust.

Without trust there is just a cold contractual relationship, one where the overheads required to maintain the relationship use more energy than any benefit derived from the association.

Just think about a manager who has a team of ten people. If the manager doesn't really trust a number of people in the team, a large percentage of that manager's personal time is spent on low-value activities – putting control systems in place, running audits and checking all the work flows and outputs. Conversely, where a manager has a trust-based relationship with all members of the team, the vast majority of the manager's time will be spent adding value and developing the capabilities of the team members.

No real surprise there. This is a common theme, but how do you learn to develop and manage trust to actively manage relationships?

The problem with trust is that it's like a good partnership – you know it when you see it, but it's hard to define the individual contribution factors. As an example, think about someone who you know well and trust implicitly. What is it that makes you think of that person? What do they and you do to maintain the relationship? Now think of another person you know just as well but don't trust. Consider what it is that each of you does to create a relationship lacking in substance and value. What's the impact of such a relationship and what overheads does it impose? If you ask them to do a job or help you out, to what extent do you have to give up valuable personal time to check and oversee the work? Do you lose sleep because there is a fear in the back of your mind that they might not deliver on time or to standard?

In many ways, the time you spend building relationships with others is an investment process, where you choose to offer and invest your personal time and capital. If you end up spending a large chunk of your time with people who actually turn out to be untrustworthy, it feels awful. Do you have relationships where this might happen? Just think, would you take a big chunk of your wages each month and place it into an account that only promised to waste your money with the result that your return is less than your investment. For me, the abuse of my personal time is as big a waste as losing money and is something I consciously guard against. Relationships are like saving accounts – we put time and energy into them in the hope that the shared success will grow and multiply, in the same way that investments in a trust fund will produce compound growth over time. Measuring your relationships might seem artificial but, like your finances, you should be aware of the amounts that you've invested in different places, monitor the levels of performance each supplier is offering and where necessary make changes to improve the return.

Managing your investment

I have a simple definition of trust that I use to measure and manage relationships:

- ◆ **Truthful** – the extent to which integrity, honesty and truthfulness are developed and maintained

- ◆ **Responsive** – the openness, mental accessibility or willingness to share ideas and information freely

- ◆ **Uniform** – the degree of consistency, reliability and predictability contained within the relationship

- ◆ **Safe** – the loyalty, benevolence or willingness to protect, support and encourage each other

- ◆ **Trained** – the competence, technical knowledge and capabilities of both parties.

Where these five attributes are soundly in place, the nature of the relationship might have the characteristics of a thick trust interaction. Conversely, where one or more of the factors is diminished or missing, it's possible the relationship is suffering from thin trust.

Leaders invest in people as well as banks
To what extent do you manage the trust levels with people you work with and care for?

In the same way that you have credits and debits with your bank, you also have a trust fund with all the people you interact with where debits and credits are applied on a daily basis.

I've seen this so clearly with my daughter Lucy as she has grown up. When Lucy first started school she found a best friend and they were sure that the relationship would stay that way for the rest of their lives – until one day this friend talked about her behind her back or told a small lie. The first time this happened they had an argument and made up. The second time it happened the relationship became strained and the third time they wandered off to find new best friends for life. The split occurred because Lucy's friend took so many withdrawals from the trust fund that it fell below the level needed to sustain a relationship.

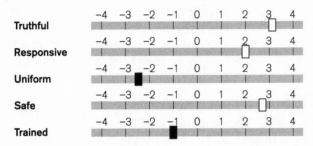

Figure 46 *Trust fund account slider*

For any relationship it's very easy for us to move the account sliders on the account into credit or debit (see Figure 46). When I run a training session I only have to tell a lie about something to weaken the truthful slider; ignore a question by someone for them to feel that I'm not being responsive; tell two people different things to upset the uniform balance; tell a story about someone else to raise concerns about how safe people feel; or appear not to be a competent trainer to reduce the value in the trained sub-account. Slippage in any one area of the trust fund erodes my personal value and even worse reduces my chance to create a shared success with the delegates on the course.

Your high is my hurt
Making deposits and withdrawing credits on your trust fund is not as easy as you might think. Just do someone a favour and you're in credit or upset them and you're in debit? But life isn't quite that simple. A while ago I managed to get some tickets to watch a key England v. Germany match on TV at our local bar (tickets were sold because of the enormous demand). I thought my sons Matt and

Michael would enjoy it. As as a great football fan, Matt was really delighted. Michael also came with us but after a while he looked uncomfortable. It turned out that he didn't really like that particular bar and would have preferred not to be there after all. In my enthusiasm to watch the match with the boys I failed to be responsive to Michael's individual needs, and what I thought was a credit turned out to be a debit. It's crucial to understand about trust funds that a credit is a credit in the eye of the receiver, not the giver.

As a further example I used to work for a firm who were keen to praise and reward people who produced quality work and at the end of the year they organized a quality award event (where people get called up on to the podium to receive a round of applause and a certificate). When I was given the honour of receiving one of these awards, I was actually mortified about parading in front of 300 people to receive it. My manager's trust fund deposit was, for me, not quite the credit he had envisaged.

Think about how you currently reward people who help you out or perform well. To what extent are you giving them credits that might be perceived as debits? Do you take people out for a beer to celebrate even if they are introverts, or do you talk to them privately when maybe they want it to be shouted from the heavens?

The challenge is to think about the credit/debit relationship, and if you really want to make a deposit in someone's trust fund, make sure you understand their map, don't impose your own.

Trust fund networks

If this seems foreboding, think about how many people in your life you value and enjoy having a relationship with. For each person you'll have a separate and unique trust fund that is either in debit or credit. Your partner, children, neighbours, work colleagues, manager, team, milkman – the list is endless and probably growing every day.

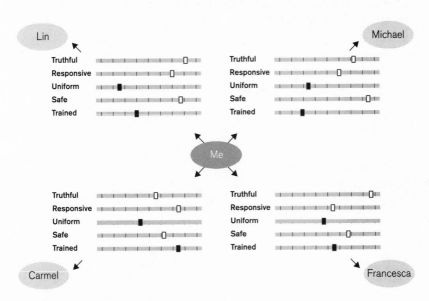

Figure 47 *Trust fund network*

Figure 47 shows a network of four people with whom I have a relationship and wish to generate shared success. My wife Lin, Michael, my son, Francesca, a treasured client, and Carmel, co-author of a book we are writing. For each of them I aspire to maintain a relationship that is always in credit, but often fail to do so. The problem occurs when conflict develops between the needs of the different players in my world. While it's important for me to spend professional time with Carmel and Francesca to develop a thick-trust relationship, it means that I give up time with Lin and Michael. This inner conflict can lead to a real problem in trying to maintain effective relationships, and also leads to increased personal turmoil. Many parents will relate to my experience of starting a new program with a new client on the same day Michael was picked to play for the school football team. The solution was a compromise aimed at maintaining some level of trust in each relationship. Lin went along and taped the match; it wasn't ideal, but I felt comfortable that it was the right decision in the circumstances.

But how can you be sure of the right decision when faced with trust fund conflict? The answer comes in the heart dimension and in particular the 'know where you're going' decision. Only when you have a clear outcome in mind can you make the hard decision about where to place your priorities and time.

Transferable trust

By managing trust, your trust fund becomes attractive to other people with a result that your account can be transferred in real time. Think about the last time you sat round a dinner table with a group of friends or went for a drink with some work colleagues. Inevitably, group conversation turns to people's opinions of absent colleagues or friends.

I guarantee that if you hear two or more people describe their experience of the same person in positive terms, their trust account will look attractive and you'll be more prepared to make an investment if you happen to meet the person.

We recently had to employ a builder to carry out some work in the house. I've been stung before by cowboy builders – they come in, mess about for a while, slap up some paint and then charge a fortune for a poor job that will only last a short while. So this time I decided to talk with the guys who own the local hardware store. I trusted them and believed that anyone they suggested would be a safe recommendation. In this sense the trust fund they have with the builder was transferred to me. The moment the builders walked in the door their trust account was already in credit (see Figure 47).

Once they started work the account sliders went into even more credit. Within five minutes I could tell that they were trained; I believed that they were telling me the truth and I felt safe enough to leave them alone in the house. The end result was that we achieved a shared success. They've been well paid for their work and I got my new wall with minimum fuss and inconvenience. And the trust

	-4	-3	-2	-1	0	1	2	3	4
Truthful								☐	
Responsive							☐		
Uniform								☐	
Safe								☐	
Trained									☐

Figure 47 *A positive trust fund*

transfer continues when I recommend them to friends. Without a positive trust fund the whole relationship would collapse and opportunities to share success would be shattered.

Once the thick trust has been attained you can start to effect success that is both shared and sustainable.

hand

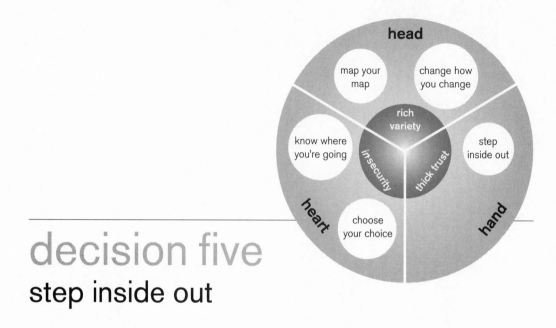

decision five
step inside out

Until you walk a mile in another man's moccasins you can't imagine the smell.

Robert Byrne

Almost as soon as Ken Livingstone became Mayor of London, he issued an edict for the London Transport chiefs to stop using their company cars and to start using public transport. He said it was only fair that those in charge of the tubes and buses should travel in them and 'share the frustration and delays'. Livingstone's edict was driven by a desire that managers should experience the frustration that passengers face and then use this understanding to improve the service and help make travel better for all.[11] In this way he was trying to realize success for the commuters by helping the managers see life from a different perspective.

Shared success is just that – the sharing of a collaborative outcome where all the players are happy with the end result. But before you can define a good end result you must know what meaning another person applies to the outcome and how they determine what shared success looks like. To do this you must step out of your universe and into theirs.

The 'step inside out' choice covers the following ideas:

◆ **Multiverse management.** We often make decisions based on the idea of a universe where our view of the world is the right view. But our world view is just one that exists in a 'multiverse', a multitude of alternative intersecting universes where an infinite number of differing versions of reality exist and interact.

◆ **3-step reframe.** This is a technique where you can step outside your view of the world and get second and third perspectives of a relationship so that you're better able to enhance how the relationship operates and as a result achieve sustainable, shared success.

◆ **Step blocks.** Moving from your universe to another is not an easy process. Along the way there will be barriers that slow you down and enablers to help you.

Multiverse management

The effective leader is able to present and frame the outcomes they need to achieve in a language and style that makes sense to the recipients. Clearly, trying to encourage a four-year-old child to keep their bedroom tidy because of the health implications might not make much sense but framing it in such a way that they understand they'll be able to make space for even more toys and have friends sleep over might make better sense.

If you see someone behaving in a way that you view as wrong or unacceptable, you have to remember that their behaviour is working for them. And once you see why it works for them and what value they get from it, you'll understand it. Then you can start to accept it and feel differently about it. To achieve this type of reframe in the way you think, feel and behave, you need to step inside out: your inner self steps out of you, and into a person with whom you wish to share success.

Let go of some of your preconceptions, assumptions and biases and start to understand what internal drivers cause other people to behave in a certain way.

For example, you might know of someone who you would describe as overbearing, directive and dictatorial. How do you react when you are with them? Is your behaviour defensive, aggressive, submissive? If you were to step inside (let's call him) Jim's body and experience, the pains and problems he faces every day, you would start to appreciate just why he appears to be such a control freak. Perhaps he lost his last job because he gave people in the team freedom to behave responsibly and with integrity, and the team abused the trust, which led to lost business and resulted in Jim's dismissal. Maybe the personal consequences of Jim's dismissal were even greater; having lost his accompanying medical benefits, his wife was moved from a private hospital to a public hospital 100 miles away from the family. As a consequence he's not prepared to be in a situation again where he offers trust to employees until he's absolutely sure that won't put his career and family life in jeopardy again. By making this leap, you start to understand what's driving others' behaviour and you can develop the right approach to bridge these problems and demonstrate that the other person can trust you.

The notion of a multiverse is crucial in any step-inside-out decision. Standing on your side of the fence you can never see someone else's problem. The first stage in understanding someone else's world view is simply acknowledging that their world exists and is related to but different to yours. You can then move on to walking in their shoes and seeing the world as they see it. But first you have to reframe your world orientation – that means taking a multidimensional view.

Reframing your world view allows you access to different perspectives and how they are formed. Reframing is an essential tool in conflict resolution and relationship management.

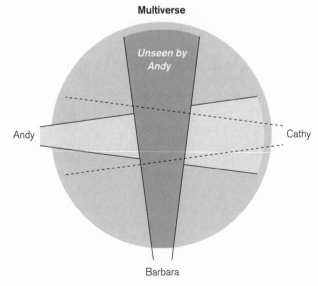

Figure 48 *The multiverse*

In Figure 49 Andy has a problem with one of his team members, Barbara. No matter how much he tries he can't seem to resolve it. He sees that her performance is down and his efforts to help don't work. But he's failed to see this from Barbara's perspective. As a single person with no commitments, Andy is driven by work, money and fun. As a single mother Barbara is driven by her family, work and rest. Unless Andy is able to step into her shoes, walk her walk and experience her life then it doesn't matter how much encouragement or extra financial inducement he offers her to improve, nothing will work. By thinking, feeling and acting as she does, he will be able to understand what factors will help to generate shared success.

3-step reframe

There are times when this book does not make sense

Maybe you agree? Or perhaps you strongly disagree. Someone flicking through this book in the bookshop will see that statement and think 'I'm not buying *that* book', but someone else will choose to buy it because they're encouraged by the fact that I put such a statement in my own book. The statement, which is common to us all, produces different thoughts, feelings and behaviours because we're all using different frames. By learning to change the frame you use to make sense of the world, you can change meaning. And when the meaning changes for you, changes in your behaviour will follow suit.

Have you ever baby sat for someone in their house? You have to reorientate yourself to a whole new set of rules. Things that you see as truths are no longer necessarily correct; in many cases, they're completely wrong. But you have to follow the other person's rules. For example, you might have brought your children up on one type of medicine but another parent might ask you to use a different type for their child. Following someone else's rules can make you feel awkward, uncomfortable and uneasy.

Now think of three people you know well but who don't have similar lifestyles to you. Be honest, to what extent could you reframe into their life and describe their universe? Could you describe what they think and worry about each day, what problems they face, or what they do each day to earn a living?

The 3-step reframe technique will help you tap into others' world views in order to answer these questions, and to move forward together to generate shared success.

The first stage of the 3-step reframe is to consider the relationship from three different perspectives: yours; the other person's; and a stranger's. The second stage is to view the relationship from different perspectives using the heart, head and hand dimensions. These two shifts are called position and dimension step reframes. By combining them into a single model you have the ability to draw out a detailed picture of your relationship with someone else.

Position steps

In the position reframe, you rotate round a relationship to gather new perspectives.

Choose a relationship and move round it taking snapshots from different directions. The first stage is to understand how the relationship looks from your perspective; then from the other person's point of view; and then from a third position where you take a snapshot in the role of detached observer (see Figure 49).

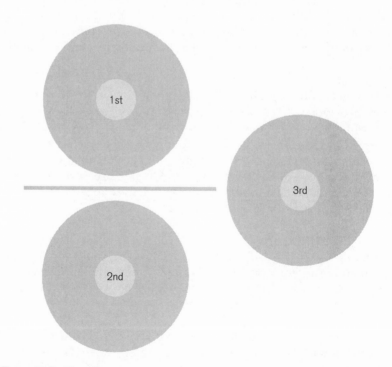

Figure 49 *Position steps*

◆ **Position 1.** Explore the relationship from your position. Look inwards and understand the current maps that you use to make sense of the world and build your universe. Understand how you view your relationship with the other person; what is happening within the relationship from your perspective and what you're doing to manage the relationship. Although in theory you'd expect to know much of this already, sometimes it can help to just sit back and ask yourself, how do I feel about this person or situation? Once you have a clear understanding of your own view of the relationship with the other person, then consciously move to the second step.

◆ **Position 2.** Move into the other person's role. Make a conscious effort to understand their universe. Try to see their problems, feel their pain, understand what daily issues they face and importantly understand how they regard the relationship with you. You should begin a shift from your universe to the other person's. You can start to get new information about the relationship. You might start to understand that what you see as supportive is perceived by others as smothering, or relaxed to you might be sloppy to them. Now, you've started to step inside out and to view a world that exists outside your own.

◆ **Position 3.** Finally, step into the role of the independent observer or dissociated commentator, who stands back from the relationship and considers what's going on between these two people. How well do they work together? What are the elements that are less effective? I've often seen this position used by directors in companies to test their strategies. Their acid test is: how would the newspapers view the strategy? A labored and tortuous strategy development process could be seen as a positive plan, or it might be put down as a failed intervention. The decision to accept or reject the strategy isn't necessarily made on the basis of such a question, but the third position acts as a safety gate to ensure that silly mistakes aren't made.

Once you've considered your relationships from all three perspectives, move back to the first position. Back at home, you can start to make decisions on what action is needed based on your new frame.

Imagine the 3-step frame in action; for instance, use it to improve the relationship with your manager. At position one, your perception is that you're not allowed any slack. Your manager doesn't give you space to take a few risks or make a name for yourself. In position two, you start to understand that what you see as her failure to let go of the reins is influenced by your failure to submit paperwork on time. In position three, step back and recognize the problem: it's less about personalities and more about management styles. You prefer to operate in a relaxed and spontaneous way; your field experience has taught you to focus on getting the job done, and paperwork comes last. Your manager prefers a structured approach; her finance background means she understands just how important it is to manage the flow of paperwork so that billing takes place on time. With all this data, step back into position one and consider what action you can take to achieve a more collaborative approach.

Dimension steps

By incorporating the head, heart and hand dimension in the process, the step-inside-out process richer. At each of the three steps, try to get information on the thoughts, feelings and behaviours in these positions (see Figure 50).

Heart steps   For example, say you want to enhance your relationship with your partner. You've had a few arguments lately and you want to understand the problem and how to resolve it. From the first

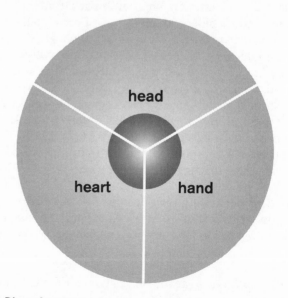

Figure 50 *Dimension steps*

position, look at why you're behaving the way you do, where the relationship is at the moment and where you believe it's heading. From a heart perspective, try and understand why you choose to feel the way you do; consider why you choose the particular responses you make to your partner's comments.

Heart questions focus on why someone is doing something and where the relationship is heading.

Move to the second position. The heart questions can be asked again. Why does your partner choose to get into the fight? Why do they respond to verbal challenges in the way they do? What do they hope to achieve from the argument? What future do they see in the relationship? Their emotional goals and drivers might be very different to yours. Ideally, at this point you should be developing an understanding of what differences exist at deep emotional levels between you and in what ways you view the future differently. The important thing here is not to focus on the arguments but to understand how each of you makes sense of your own universe.

In the third position, imagine yourself sitting in a cinema watching a film of these two people fighting. Why are they arguing? Are their arguments about a real issue, or are they a symptom of their desire to achieve different life goals? Have they taken time to share their goals and desires with each other or are they held in darkness? Are they willing to make real choices about the argument, and do they have the inner security to resolve the problem in a position of strength?

Head steps   Using the head perspective, the questions are about defining and understanding what maps people are using, how they differ, and what approach is being taken to resolve problems.

Imagine that you're in a position where the relationship with your manager is breaking down. Over recent months you've been arguing, niggling each other and generally failing to agree on the way that problems might be resolved. You've decided that the position is untenable, both for you and the other members of the team, who have to deal with the fallout.

In the first position you need to understand your own map. Consider how you see the current situation, what you find acceptable and unacceptable. Have you climbed the fantasy ladder? What are the real facts? Use any of the topics covered in the map-your-map section to gain clarity over how you view the situation.

Understanding the other person's map is the objective in the second position. What degree of variety do they have in the way they look at things? What do they view as acceptable and unacceptable? What is their standard operating procedure? Do they view you as an individual or as just another member of their team? And what shadow maps are operating? In essence, how do they make sense of the world and how do they view their relationship with you?

Finally, view the situation from a detached position. If you were to read a similar story in the newspaper, who would you say is to blame? Where do the two people share similar ideas and where do they differ? To what extent is there a way of thinking that will satisfy both their needs? Once you've commented on the relationship from the third position, step back to the first position and respond to your advice.

Hand steps   In hand reframe you try to experience the physical environment of the other person. A hand reframe for a managing director might be to work with the customer service people for a while to understand the problems they have when dealing with irate customers. Or, a member of the customer service team could spend a day covering the manager's position to get a feel for the problems of senior management.

Vinnie Jones is a good example of a successful hand reframe. Vinnie Jones, the Watford-born footballer of Wimbledon and Wales, concluded a successful career in football to try his hand at acting. After a highly successful appearance in *Lock, Stock and Two Smoking Barrels*, he made the jump into acting as a full-time profession. One of his first decisions was to repatriate himself and his family to Hollywood. After he made the choice to become a film star he recognized that 'if you're serious about acting then Hollywood is the place to be. You have to be physically present in the place where the action is happening.' This is so you understand how the film world operates from first-hand experience and meet the right people. He said, 'I'm getting to know people and I'm getting known and that's what it's all about.'[12]

I had a much less glamorous experience one week when I stepped out of my usual frame and helped the boys with their paper round. Michael and Matt had been doing the paper round for a couple of years. Every Wednesday the papers would be delivered to our house and they would insert advertising leaflets ready for delivery on Thursday. I had some free time so I thought I would help them out. Unfortunately, the week I chose to help was cold, raining and blowing up a real gale. I told them my stories of when I used to be a paperboy and go out in 'weather that was ten times worse than this!'. I thought I knew it all. But I soon ate my words. I couldn't believe how many houses had small yappy dogs whose only passion in life is to attack your fingertips when you push the paper through, and they're ably helped by modern-day post flaps – their large coil springs have enough torque to raise the Titanic. It takes Herculean strength just to open the flap, and then once your fingers are in they jam shut just above the knuckles so the dog can get them. The papers weigh a ton and the the gardens have all sorts of lethal obstacles – broken gates, wonky paving, and thorny bushes. With my souvenirs of the day – a twisted ankle, sore fingers and damaged pride – I realized I'd far sooner face a baying crowd of angry executives than have a paper round these days.

Sometimes we really have to get our hands dirty and physically experience what others go through in order to understand their part in a relationship.

3-step reframe: position and dimension

The real power of reframing using the different dimensions comes when you're able to step into each position and consider it with all three dimensions (see Figure 51).

With any problem which you wish to resolve in a relationship, look at it from all angles. Use the following sets of questions as a guide:

In the first position, consider:

◆ How do I feel about this relationship?

◆ Where do I believe it's heading?

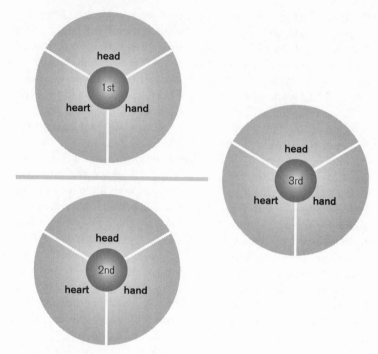

Figure 51 *3-step reframe*

◆ What do I think is right and wrong with it?

◆ How have I tried to resolve the problem, for example, with subtlety, spontaneity or in an open and planned way?

In the second position:

◆ How do I feel about the other person (me, that is)?

◆ How are we behaving towards each other?

◆ Why do I think this is happening?

◆ How would I like the other person to behave?

◆ How would I feel if they changed?

◆ What would I do in response?

In the third position (the independent view), ask:

◆ How are these people behaving towards each other?

- How do I feel about their behaviour?
- Is either of them in the wrong?
- Why do I think this is happening?
- What advice would I give to the first person to help them improve the relationship?

Once you've completed the 3-step reframe process, reflect on the insights that the other positions have offered and try to effect a real solution that will enhance the relationship.

Step dynamics

OK, so the theory seems quite simple: just put yourself in the other person's shoes and all is well. Not quite. People like being where they are and don't like to move to positions that are unnatural for them. And if you ask them to step into the role of someone they don't get along with or don't like, the barriers really come up and in many cases people just refuse. It's this refusal and unwillingness to see the world from another person's perspective that leads to problems in the first place.

Step barriers
If you're to operate on the principle of shared success, then a number of logical, physical and emotional blockages need to be managed and overcome so that you are able see another person's point of view.

◆ **Legacy experiences.** Our past experiences can distort our view. We have a video recorder in our head that has a stock-pile of film clips that can instantly replay that bad or embarrassing moment we had with someone years ago. So you need to develop the ability to archive the film clips. You don't have to erase past incidents, just learn to put them to one side while you try to live in their universe.

◆ **Bias.** Communication between people is frequently distorted when one person decides in advance that the other isn't worth listening to. Imagine the West Ham footballer who's asked to understand the universe a Tottenham supporter lives in. The instant response is 'No way'. Years of conditioning and bias kick in and a barrier to the step-inside-out process is erected. This can be seen in work all the time as tribal walls are established between functional or regional groups. The northerners hate the southerners, and vice versa; the engineers hate the sales reps. If you are to manage the step-inside-out process, you must catch this bias and put it in temporary storage before it blocks your ability to effect a change.

- **Status.** Perhaps the most difficult barrier to overcome in making the shift is status. Any difference in status power, authority or position can make the shift difficult. It can be hard to understand how someone else acquires and employs their power base. Do they use the status as a foil to drive and effect change in an open and discussable way, or is it a shadow factor, where their power is inferred and managed as a backstage operation?

Enabling strategies

However, there are certain simple strategies that can be employed to enable the process.

- **No one makes a bad decision.** This is possibly the most difficult mental switch to make. Think about the statement, 'no one makes a bad decision'. Everyone, whoever they are, makes the best possible decision that they can at any particular moment in time. This is the colleague who decided to usurp your authority and set up a program office in a different location, or the teenager who decided to take drugs. To you, they might be decisions that you don't agree with, but at the instant the decision was made it was the right one for them. Based on all the data, recourses and evidence, they made a choice. They might regret it later, but at that moment it was their best possible decision. If you can't accept this principle, you'll be entering someone else's universe through a critical frame rather than an enquiring one and blockages will exist from the outset.

- **Live the context.** Wherever possible, try to adopt the second position in the environment the other person operates in. If you're a managing director who wants to develop an appreciation of problems at the coalface, you could think yourself into the role of engineer or sales agent, but it's unlikely that you'll appreciate the detail of the problems they face on a daily basis without stepping into the context in which they work.

- **Manage the inner voice.** One of the difficulties with stepping into a secondary or third position is that your inner voice still has a say over how you think, feel and behave. In an ideal world you would close the inner voice down and focus on the voice of the person whose shoes you're walking in. However, the reality is that it takes an amazing amount of will power and personal control to shut down this internal stream of thoughts. One of the ways to overcome this is not to try to close the voice down, but just accept that the inner voice is challenging the second and third position thoughts; have a dialogue with it from these positions. What you're doing is taking a viewpoint different to your own and reinforcing your transition to your new position by arguing with yourself.

◆ **Go third first.** Imagine you want to build a relationship with someone at work who you find really irritating. You might understand the need to step inside out but the thought of taking their view of the world feels absolutely appalling. Try jumping straight into the third position. Look at the relationship from a detached position. Once you've stepped into the relatively safe, objective, position it then becomes much easier to move to the second position.

◆ **Separate the relationship from the person.** When in the second position, try to think about the individual in whose shoes you're walking, don't initially focus on how they feel about their relationship with you. The essence of the step-inside-out choice is to understand the person first, then, once you understand the individual's drivers, their relationship with you. If you immediately focus on how they interact with you, it makes it more difficult to separate yourself.

These techniques may help but to really find the most effective way for you to step to the second and third positions, you'll need to practise, and in doing so develop your own strategies and styles.

Step inside out: quick summary

◆ It's very difficult to step inside out and see the world from someone else's perspective. You like being where you are and don't like to move to an unnatural position. But your inability or unwillingness to see the world from the other person's position reduces the chance to share success.

◆ You often make decisions based on the idea of a single universe: your own. You have to accept that your world view isn't the only one and that other people's views are equally valid. Your universe is just one with countless others that form a multiverse.

◆ No one makes a bad decision or does the wrong thing. If you see someone behaving in a way that you think is wrong or unacceptable you have to accept that the behaviour they've chosen works for them.

◆ Behaviour changes with context and will have a totally different meaning, value and outcome. As a leader, your role is to appreciate the many different meanings you can apply to what people do, think and feel.

◆ Effective leaders always present ideas and outcomes in a style that makes sense to others.

◆ To overcome the fantasy gap created by different legacy and value systems, you must be able to step inside the other person's shoes and understand their maps using the 3-step reframe.

◆ The 3-step reframe requires two changes. First shift yourself into another person's universe and see life from their perspective. Second, understand the other person's viewpoint via the heart, head and hand dimensions.

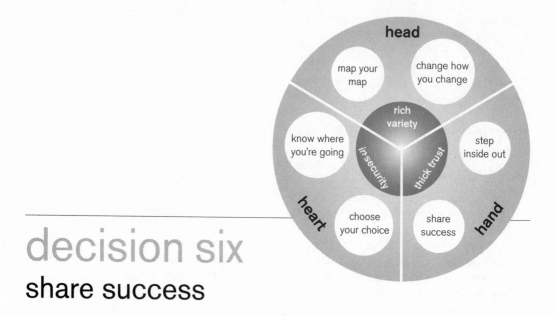

decision six
share success

Coming together is the beginning. Keeping together is progress.
Working together is success.

Henry Ford

As you reach a position where you have control over the first five choices in the personal leadership framework, you might find that there's a fine line between being self-confident and being selfish. By having control over your life, you might appear to ignore or override other people's needs. Using your personal power solely to achieve the things you desire will undo the benefits accrued so far.

Personal leadership that is selfish and short-lived is not true success.

The only real form of personal leadership is one founded on the notion of shared and sustainable outcomes and the key to this choice is the absolute focus on mutual benefit.

Shared success is about using the following tools:

◆ **advocacy and inquiry** – the ability to tell others what we expect of them and ask them what they expect of us

◆ **thinking 'compound'** – the idea that good begets great, and great begets excellent

◆ **the values bridge** – the alignment of our values, our value and feeling valued.

Advocacy and inquiry

You can only achieve shared success if you understand what success means for you and others. I see people working together to achieve a shared outcome but they don't really understand what the other person wants to achieve. The end result teeters between a battle of wills as each person struggles to assert their view of success, or lacklustre output because no one has really said what is important for them. If we assume that everyone is different and has distinct goals and ambitions, then we can understand what real success is for the people we work and live with.

Well, it worked for me, so it must work for you!
I've worked in many teams that had larger than life, extrovert managers who, when they come to reward the people in the team, follow a reward pattern that aligns with their view of the world. This might be to take people down to the pub for a big party, put the person's name in banners around the room or publish their success in the company newsletter. This is fine if you're someone who shares those extrovert preferences, but if you're anything like me, more of an introvert, this type of reward is unsettling; I've found it actually reduced my desire to improve on the results next time round. Though with the best of intentions, the manager believes they are sharing their success, in fact they're operating on the basis of a selfish success principle.

But it isn't the manager's fault if the rewards they think people will value are based on their own preferences. As individuals, we have a say in the matter and a responsibility to be courageous, if that's what it takes, to tell them our preferences and how we'd like to be rewarded. The only way to share success is to operate a push–pull system. A push strategy ensures that others will understand what success means to you, and a pull strategy means you can take time out to understand what success will be for them:

◆ **advocacy** – making sure other people know what you want and need by having the courage to tell them.

◆ **inquiry** – understanding other people's goals, dreams and desires, by showing consideration and seeking to understand what success means for them.

Once you understand these two dimensions you can appreciate how they interrelate and what the consequences are when they are observed in a relationship.

As these two dimensions interact we can realize four different types of success (see Figure 52):

◆ **selfish** – this is high advocacy and is an appropriate strategy when you have to fight a raging fire. I see this in senior managers who have to rescue a company that has a problem but don't have time to negotiate solutions – they have to set a direction and head for it fast. However, once in this position, you risk not being able to step into a different segment.

◆ **squandered** – the result of low advocacy and inquiry skills. You'll see this in committee meetings where people just turn up because the diary says there's a meeting – it means the companies' resources, including its managers' time, are squandered.

◆ **subordinate** – where you've spent too much time inquiring what success will be for someone else and too little time on what you want out of the relationship. As a parent, you often find yourself seeing to everyone else's needs and subordinating your own; it generally isn't the most productive thing to do as you're spreading your time and talents too thinly, and in the end, no one benefits fully from your efforts, especially you.

◆ **shared** – achieving a balance between: strength and courage to set out just what's important for you; and enough consideration and care to listen to others. This requires genuine listening, not just polite nods and smiles. Unless you're engaged and listening with your heart and your head, you'll never understand what success really means for the people you're with.

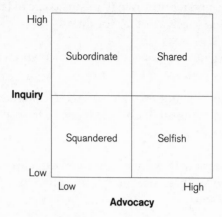

Figure 52 *Shared success matrix*

Think 'compound'

Success has a wide bandwidth of possibilities. The resolution of a political debate in Parliament is usually viewed as a success. But is this true when the solution is a fudge to get it through the legislative and political process? And does this really draw upon the politician's capabilities to enhance the lives of their constituents? The final bill might simply be a political compromise that satisfies the base needs of each party but doesn't really help transform and resolve some of the deeper problems that weaken society. What's missing is a sense of collaboration and synergistic thinking that takes people's deeper ideas and beliefs and transforms them into something new and original.

Yet another fight in the studio!
Every time I record a new CD, there is some form of negotiation and trade-off between the members of the band. Whose songs do we record? Who takes the solo break? Who sings? And so on. The whole experience is one long stream of negotiated debate that can and often does turn into argument (physical fights one reserved for the most glamorous bands!). Yet our whole objective during the recording and production processes is to avoid compromise and make do. Our goal is to ensure that the relationship operates at a compound level because the true worth of a relationship comes from the ability to create something from nothing.

Like investing a pound in a high deposit account and watching it grow effortlessly, investment in compound relationships gives a good return.

This is a really important part of the shared success quadrant (see Figure 54). So often people invest in relationships that process nothing

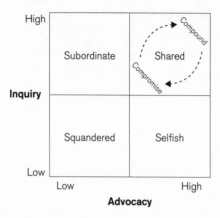

Figure 53 *Compound investment*

more than the sum of the parts. If you choose to spend time with someone on a project, you're giving away valuable time, energy and ideas. You can't afford to give such resources away if the relationship is going to operate at a level of compromise. Instead, you want to work with people who take your ideas and build on them and whose ideas you can build on in turn. The net result is a compound or synergistic relationship, where the sum of the parts is greater than the whole.

This is such a simple idea but one that people often fail to think about. Most people wouldn't even consider investing their hard earned money in a savings account where the end of year return was the same amount of money. When we invest our personal cash we trust the bank to invest the money wisely in the market and to return interest on a compound basis.

Compound success is founded on two principles. *Exposed Advocacy*, where you're prepared to expose your deep personal success criteria and share them with other people; and *Empathic Inquiry* where your goal is to use an inquiry structure that enables the other person to expose their inner personal success criteria. Where both principles are employed a shift is made from compromise to compound success (see Figure 54).

Exposed advocacy
Advocacy is about putting forth a personal idea or feeling in order to stimulate a specific outcome. In his book *The Fifth Discipline*, Peter

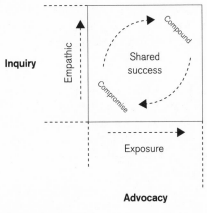

Inquiry

Empathic

Shared success

Compound

Compromise

Exposure

Advocacy

Figure 54 *Compound success*

Senge suggests that advocacy is the ability to solve problems by enlisting support, winning arguments and getting things done. It is a head-based process where you present data or logical thought. The head dimension is employed to filter data in and out of the positioning argument in order to ensure that a win is achieved. However, exposed advocacy is a process where you attempt to expose your deep feelings and values to other people to help realize an outcome that satisfies a deeper set of ambitions and needs. The idea is to retain the head function but to achieve a sustained shared success based on shared values, principles and deep desires.

To manage the process of exposed advocacy you must:

- **expose private wins** – have a clear and focused understanding of what good means to you. How would you define success from your perspective and how can you make it clear enough for others to understand?

- **discuss undiscussables** – the essence of exposed advocacy is to surface the shadow desires, to feel comfortable enough to expose and explain the deep personal factors that really drive your behaviour to another person

- **welcome debate** – offer the recipients the chance to explore and understand the ideas being put forward. Unless the other person feels able to explore the success factors you're aiming for, there is a chance they won't fully understand what the aims are and how they can be achieved.

hand

lead yourself

momentum

So that shared success does not fall into selfish success where your effort is one sided with your needs taking pole position, Exposed Advocacy should be balanced by Empathic Inquiry.

Empathic Inquiry

You probably think you're a good listener. But how good are you at empathic listening, where the skill is to inquire about the other's person goals by helping to make the unconscious conscious? Inquiry is a formal process to take in information, whereas empathic listening is about listening with the heart without the need to impose your personal interpretations.

Empathic Inquiry means you must:

- **decide to listen.** This might sound silly, but it's the conscious desire to put the tacit receptors into gear and to listen with your heart. This is a very specific and conscious process, not something that simply happens as you're walking along the corridor chatting with someone.

- **minimize internal distractions.** Develop a sense of rapport and put your own needs, thoughts and values temporarily aside. As we listen to other people describe their goals it's easy for the inner voice to jump in and challenge or disagree with the statement being made. Your inner voice must be tightly managed to ensure it doesn't corrupt the inflow of thoughts and feelings from the other person.

- **love paradox.** You must be able to agree with the speaker's wish to achieve a set of goals, even if you don't agree with the actual goals. This is the art of listening without prejudice and accepting other people's wishes without acting as critic.

- **clarify on line.** As you manage the inquiry process, you will stimulate a flow of thoughts and feelings from the other person. While this data is flowing inwards you must be able to reflect back and check for understanding.

- **manage air space.** You must stay conscious to the balance between listening and telling as there is always competition for air space. Try to ensure that the balance is appropriate for the outcome you wish to achieve.

If you can reach a stage where both players in a relationship are able to offer both empathic inquiry and exposed advocacy, you have a genuine and successful relationship. This is where generative learning is being used to help people genuinely understand what shared success might look like and agree how to realize compound shared success.

Imagine you manage a small team of customer service operators in a busy call center. You've managed the team for the past two years and have a good working relationship with all the members. Two weeks ago Pete, a new member, transferred from a different office to join the team. All went well in the first few days, but at the end of the first week tension emerged. Pete wanted to set up a small project team to review the office procedures, but you felt there was little need for this as the team was functioning well already. You eventually agreed a middle ground. Pete would undertake a personal review of the procedures but not take up the valuable time of any of the other team members.

However, a few days later, Pete published his findings without your agreement. The result was that the divisional manager became involved and started to question why changes were being proposed to the procedures without her agreement. You face a dilemma: should you take Pete to one side and really lay down the law as to the expected behaviours within the team; or should you try to understand what deeper issues were being played out in the team? Using the idea of empathic inquiry and exposed advocacy, you arrange to spend some time with Pete to try and agree how you can best work together. Rather than telling Pete how he should approach his job, you try to understand why he took the action he did and what he'd hoped to achieve by running the project.

After a while it turns out that Pete is paying to put himself through a degree school at evening class. He's spent many years at the same level in the organization, but has decided to seek promotion and he sees the move to your team as part of this journey. Now you can understand why Pete was behaving in such a way and why he'd felt the need to make a splash. Once this was clear, you took some time to explain your own personal goals and how things are in the team. You explained that you were plannning to start a family and were contemplating a career break. Once both of you understood the deeper personal issues, it became relatively simple to find an outcome that would be successful and sustainable (see Figure 55). You agree that Pete can wherever possible take greater responsibility

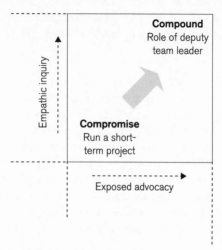

Figure 55 *Compound outcome*

for high-profile projects that come into the team. In return, you can reduce the amount of evening and weekend work that you were doing and spend time preparing the house for the new arrival. The original shared success could have worked but was not really satisfying and sustainable. The final solution is an agreement that satisfies real personal criteria.

Take it to the limit
The shift from compromise to compound success is based on your ability and desire to take the advocacy and inquiry dimensions to the limit.

If the relationship isn't reaching its full potential, are you really using the full power of exposed advocacy and empathic inquiry?

Is all your energy and passion focused on extracting from the other person their personal success criteria and helping them understand your own?

The highest level of interaction is one where the communication between groups of people results in compound outcomes, and the amplification of people's ideas. As people expose their thoughts, ideas and personal patterns, so the level of understanding and knowledge within the room will expand. This type of approach needs to happen in scenario or business planning workshops, where the interaction between people will create new ideas, themes and patterns that might not have existed before the event. However, to ensure that the ideas are new from within the group and not just a compromise, there needs to be a concerted effort from all parties to focus on the give-and-take aspects within the relationships.

hand

lead yourself

momentum

The V-ness factors

The ability to share success is often driven by the hidden factors in a relationship, the V-ness factors (see Figure 56). These are:

◆ the extent to which you share the same **values** and beliefs as the others in the relationship

◆ the extent to which care and consideration are demonstrated, with the result that people feel **valued**

◆ the extent to which you demonstrate that you understand the **value** the other person adds to the relationship.

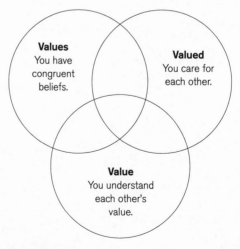

Figure 56 *The V-ness factors*

These three variables offer a significant contribution to the success of any relationship, and failure to deal with any of the factors limits the opportunity to share success.

Values

At the heart of any organization, family or social group are the values of the individuals who make up the culture. It's these personal and shared beliefs that bind people together, push them apart, and generally make the world go round. We must therefore be sure that the values of the people, teams and organization are related in such a way as to facilitate success.

Espoused versus real values. People rarely take the time to appraise critically and understand what their values are and how they relate to the notion of shared success. Bear in mind that when considering people's values, though there might be visible clues, there are also many hidden facets and issues that can't be inferred from observation. This raises a number of important issues in relation to the use of values if we wish to share success:

◆ The values that people display may not be what they feel inside.

◆ Espoused values might not be the ones that drive the person or the organization.

◆ The paradox of conforming to organizational values while aspiring to maintain one's own values can result in defence routines. This creates the falsification of behaviours and actions to simply satisfy the organization's social and political system.

Shared success can only be realized when there is alignment between the individual's and the organization's value set. It should be an overriding goal of any organization to discover and capture as much as possible of the value that is held within its people, and within this diversity of values should be positive discovery.

Cross the values bridge. We need to create a pincer movement to understand others' (friends', manager's, partner's, etc.) beliefs and values and to be prepared to offer our view of what we value and hold dear. No longer is it possible for the communication of company values to be a brainwashing process.[13] The objective is to create a shared mindset, one that can help to create a common sense of resonance, even across diverse and varied value sets.

Bridge building is the crucial ability to manage the integration of what might be vastly differing value sets. Any political party wanting to move in a new direction has to take on board a new set of beliefs and values brought to the surface by the addition of new members. Initially conflict and confusion arise as members try to come to terms with a new set of norms and beliefs. Within this process people will generally ask two questions: which of my current beliefs will I concede to take on this new way of working? and, which of my core values should I retain as sacrosanct?

The values bridge (Figure 57) shows how you can manage different values by taking the value that someone else has espoused and mapping it with the values you hold important. To do this takes a degree of maturity because it's built on the principle that shared success can in many cases only be achieved by giving up certain strongly held beliefs and ideals. For each person you need to first understand what their values are, then prioritize them. Finally, the goal is to understand the other person's hierarchy of values and then build a bridge between the two value sets so that both understand those areas you're both prepared to concede, and to clearly suggest what isn't negotiable and can't be shifted.

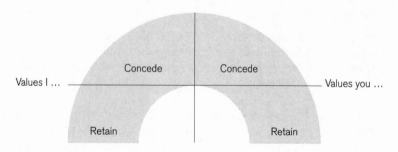

Figure 57 *The values bridge*

Stretch the values bandwidth. Once you both understand the boundaries you're operating within, it's easier to manage the boundaries and start to accept and operate under someone else's value set. This approach is known as values bandwidth management (see Figure 59). The objective of this approach is to allow people to understand and adapt to each other's value sets within a managed framework. This means that value differences can be managed and provide a vehicle by which people can share success on their own terms.

Imagine two people who have started to work together on a new time-critical project. They get along well but realize they have quite differing views on the right and wrong way to work in a difficult situation. One of them might believe that when the chips are down then it's right to ignore the family commitments and focus entirely on work. The other person believes that work is only part of their life and has a personal commitment to be home at night to put the children to bed and read them a story. There is little chance that these two people will agree because of their entrenched and absolute beliefs. But it might be that they can identify some points of flex and operate in the concede area of bandwidth ('a' in Figure 58). It might turn out that they're both happy to work on Saturday morning in order to meet the tight deadline because this doesn't run counter to their beliefs and commitments. After some time and discussion they might move to bandwidth 'b' and realize that the trust fund is sufficiently high that they don't need to be in the office together to work on the project, so maybe they can work at home. Finally, they may move to bandwidth 'c' where they both respect and understand the other's values and are prepared to find shared success that will deliver the outcome without giving up their beliefs.

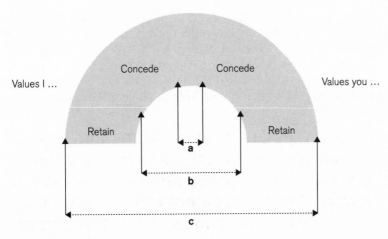

Figure 58 *Values bridge bandwidth management*

The most difficult aspect of the values bridge is the notion that you should concede in areas you hold dear. However, the goal is to be pragmatic, not submissive. I might decide that all my values are dear to me and that I'm not prepared to give up any of them – the chances that there might be someone in this life who has a value set that exactly matches my own will be rare – and so there's every chance I'll die a sad and lonely old devil. It's right to have a set of core values that you hold on to and don't let go of no matter what. But it also makes sense to have a set that are important but negotiable.

To make the values bridge work you have to ask youself three questions:

◆ Do you know what my values are in priority order?
◆ Do you know others' values in priority order?
◆ To what extent are you prepared to give and take in order to achieve shared success?

I know of many situations where a failure to address these issues has resulted in problems for the individual and the company where they work. I met one group of people who worked for a company that was founded on a set of core values. These values were used to bind the group together as they grew and went though difficult times and each new recruit was selected to match the values. All was well until a change in leadership occurred and the values that had been lived right from the outset changed. The end result is that almost an entire team left the business over a short period.

They felt that the company no longer understood the values that were important and non-negotiable to them and they had no choice but to leave. The use of the values bridge might not have prevented the mass departure, but it would have offered a vehicle by which people could talk about their feelings and how their personal priorities were being disregarded.

To what extent are you aware of your values and the values of the people you live and work with? To what extent do you discuss these values and how they impact on your relationships? To what extent are you prepared to give way on your ideals and correspondingly require others to give way on theirs?

Valued

What is it that makes you give the best of yourself in a task? What is it that makes you go that extra mile to make a relationship work that bit better? What is it that makes you want to work with someone a second or third time even if the previous projects didn't quite deliver all that was expected? It's often because you feel that the person, team or organization appreciate you and the work you put into a task.

One simple example is that of a schoolteacher called Eric Watson. One day Eric received a phone call and the caller said: 'This is James Smith ... you taught me at school 16 years ago. I'm in the area on holiday and knowing you lived around here thought I'd like to take you out to dinner.' Throughout the dinner Eric couldn't but wonder why James was wining and dining him. At the coffee stage he commented on the delightful meal and then came the answer. Rather shyly James said, 'I've got a very good job. I'm a mechanical engineer and it's all down to you. Your science lessons got me interested, not just because of the actual lesson, but your enthusiasm. Science lessons were the highlight of the day, and this is my way of saying thank you.' Eric reflected afterwards how he survives the constant problem of bullies, changing work schemes and new systems, and came to one conclusion: the old-fashioned occasional apple from a grateful pupil. In the same way that a teacher enjoys feeling valued by the children and the system, we all need to feel valued by the recipients of our efforts.[14]

The smile that says a thousand words. If you've ever performed in a band, played sports for an audience, performed in a play or worked on a checkout till in the supermarket, you know how soul-destroying it can be to receive negative feedback or sometimes, even worse, no feedback. Often all it needs is one person to smile and say thank you, clap with enthusiasm or shout your name out with pride at the end of the performance to make it all worth while.

People do better when they feel better, and people feel better when they're given positive feedback and personal reinforcement.

How often do you give positive feedback when people deserve it? Do you just assume they know they've done OK? It still amazes me just how often people go through a supermarket checkout without offering any warmth or feedback to the person stuck behind the till. This poor person is jammed in a space smaller than a stair cupboard, receiving low pay and dealing with all sorts of clientele, and yet nearly everyone I meet always has a smile and will help cheer up my day. It really jars when people walk through and can't be bothered to offer the smallest thank you or polite goodbye. Even worse is the pseudo thank you said with no link to the heart dimension. The only way to make people feel really valued for their efforts is to use all three dimensions, head, hand *and* heart. You have to know with your heart why you're saying thank you and use your whole body to demonstrate that it's a real and genuine, personal, thank you.

Just what is the cost of a thank you? How often do your manager, partner, colleagues or friends really make you feel valued for something you've done? Or, to look at that question another way: How often do you truly make other people feel valued for the effort they put into something for you? The picture your child painted for you, the extra hours overtime that your team member put in on a Saturday morning, or the fact that your partner brought you a coffee in bed – do you really make time to look for these efforts and read them with your heart? Or have you become oblivious to it all? Even as I write these words I think back on the times that I've been working in the office and one of the children has brought me a picture they'd painted for me. Though I often responded with a head and hand response, saying and doing the right things, in reality my heart was not involved in the interaction. I was still focused on the paper I was working on. The sad thing is, I can never have those moments again. They're lost – and that is such a waste.

It's within the power of all of us to give strokes of recognition to those we want to feel valued.

It costs nothing but delivers rewards that seal relationships, and can help deliver sustainable shared success. Strokes are in essence a unit or statement of recognition. Some strokes are positive and some are negative. Some strokes are driven by the hand dimension. This might be a touch on the shoulder to say thank you or a round of applause at the end of a presentation. Some might be head-based and driven by an intellectual recognition of effort. This might be an e-mail to say thank you or a write up in the in-house magazine.

Others might be heart-based where you sit down with someone and tell them how you really feel about the effort they've made. Even when the strokes have a primary dimension, it's important that they contain some element of all three factors of head, hand and heart; without this the stroke will feel false and soulless.

There is a downside to this idea of valued strokes, and that is the 'professional thanker'. These are the people who have just been on a customer service course or a 'How to get the best from your people' program. They arrive back home or in the office with a huge smile and full of a desire to reward everyone every time they do something, every minute of the day. No matter what you do they'll find a way to thank you for your efforts. They end up like the game show host smiling and loving everyone, but often underneath they're still the same old person. I don't wish to undervalue such programs, but just make you aware. If someone's natural orientation isn't naturally to show how much they genuinely value you, just going on a course won't change their embedded behaviour. It will change the hand, it might change the head, but, deep down, change to the heart takes longer and needs time and support to be sustainable.

Value
Consider the human instrument as something that interfaces with the world. As we interact with the environment we make different types of exchanges. We take in oxygen and give out carbon dioxide; we take in food and water and give out waste to be reprocessed; we take in information, process it, possibly add some value and then pass on that knowledge in return for some personal benefit.

The currency of personal capital. We trade our personal capital as a form of soft currency. We pay money to read someone else's book and use this information to write a paper at work; we attend a course to gain parenting skills to help our children grow; or we pay to see a play that will give us insight into someone else's emotional view of the world, and use this experience to build a better relationship with a friend or colleague.

If we look at these examples, they fall into three currency groups: we exchange currency or value with the world in terms of how we think (head), act (hand) or feel (heart). In the vast majority of cases we draw on all three currencies to create value in the market. Though all three might be used to deliver a single product, it's likely that one of them will take a dominant role.

As a musician my dominant factor is a hand currency because my added value comes from the skills of playing the guitar. As an author the dominant factor is head currency because I am presenting you my ideas and mental tools. And much of my market value as a consultant comes from the heart currency and my ability to create effective emotional relationships with my clients. Now this isn't to suggest that the people who watch me play in the local bar don't value my emotions as I play or my ability to know what notes to play. The core added value is around the capability to play the guitar and the other currencies help position it in the market. When we consider all three areas, we can understand how we use the idea of head, hands and heart currencies to trade with the world.

Don't blame others for not recognizing your value. Think about some of the primary activities you undertake in your life – parent, schoolteacher, manager, sportsperson, and so on – where you have to produce a shared output with another person, team or organization. Take each one and consider its component parts in terms of head, hand and heart (see Figure 59).

For each element, think about the value you're contributing to others and consider whether you're satisfied that you're getting the rewards you deserve. The currency might be monetary if you're working for a company, or emotional thanks when you've done something for your partner or your child. If, in your actions, there's an imbalance between the three dimensions, and even though your intention is altruistic, it might be that you cherish the payment too much – that treasured smile from your partner or your child's simple thank you.

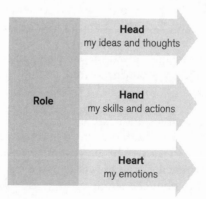

Figure 59 *Value currency*

If this is the case, and recognition is one of the primary motivators for you, performing acts of kindness and not necessarily getting what you feel is the right response will mean you develop inner tension or simply withdraw your efforts or favours because you feel uncomfortable and under-valued.

An obvious example of this is in a work situation. We've all been there. You've just spent hours and hours at home over the weekend trying to finish off a report or stopped behind at work for a while to tidy up the bench. When this isn't recognized by the company, it's irritating and leads to frustration and a withdrawal of work effort the next time you're called on to help out. But it's the type of reaction that limits your chance to share success because the frustration and anger will always come out in some form or another.

People often blame the company and bemoan the fact that their efforts haven't been recognized or valued. Nonsense! The onus is on you to map, measure, manage and market your personal value.

It's not their responsibility to pamper and comfort you. It's your personal capital so it behoves you to place a value on it and ensure that you receive a fair and suitable reward from the market. This type of mentality is the same as a high street shop blaming the customers for not shopping with them. At the end of the day it's a question of supply and demand – you have products that the company needs: realize the value or find someone else who will. If you don't have products that the company needs now or in the future, get some! Or beware the next rounds of downsizing.

If you believe you're not receiving a fair and equitable reward for your effort, distraction and disquiet will set in and erode the sustainability of success.

Robert Louis Stevenson said, 'Everyone lives by selling something.' So, ask yourself: What do I trade with the world to create success? Do I determine its market value? Do others place the same value on my capital? This point is critical because imbalanced reward will limit any chances you have of repeating your successes.

V-ness imbalance

Some people are unable to share success, not because they don't use the ideas in the V-ness model, but because they have different preferences and strengths in each of the three areas.

For example a colleague of mine had a problem where a sudden change in V-ness balance caused her to rethink her position within a company and ultimately to leave. When she first joined the company, it was a small fledgling business that was driven by all three V-ness factors. Of the three factors, the roots of the business were founded in the core values but there was also a shared desire to earn a decent wage and maximize a return on their personal value in the market. Although the 'valued' factor was important as they often operated as free agents, their need for peer feedback and strokes of recognition was minimal because people were happy to pick up on this whenever they met for a social lunch or team meeting.

As the company started to grow at a rapid rate, it developed a strong brand in the market and reached a point where it had quadrupled in size. A new management team was formed with the goal of taking the business into a new phase of strategic and operational success. At this point the V-ness factor changed. The shift from a values-based culture moved toward a cost-based style of operating. From the senior team's point of view this made sense – so many new people meant they had to guarantee future income streams. However, for this person the values driver was still strong and something started to feel wrong. She couldn't necessarily explain what it was, but she knew that the level of her internal discomfort meant that it was time to leave.

Now, this tale doesn't exist in isolation. We all know of other people who have become disillusioned, left the company, divorced, lost friends because of the same subtle shift in the V-ness balance. The main problem is when the shift is subtle or imperceptible. If a problem happens within an organization or relationship in an unambiguous way, the shift can be discussed openly and people can make choices about their future. When the shift takes place over time, it's not discussed in an open forum and deceit, bad feeling and apathy filter into the relationships.

The challenge for us all is to be sensitive to the balance of the V-ness factors. We need to be tuned into our preferences, the preferences of others and the environment in general. If there is an imbalance or conflict across our values, how we feel valued, and how we reward value, it must be understood so that the option to share success is managed and remains sustainable.

Share success: quick summary

◆ Personal leadership that is selfish and short-lived is not true success. The only real form of personal leadership is one founded on the notion of shared outcomes and sustainable performance.

◆ At the heart of your ability to share success is the need to understand and align the V-ness factors: values; feeling valued; and personal value.

◆ The extent to which you feel valued by your partner, manager or company can make a huge difference in your willingness to give a little more.

◆ The onus is on you to promote your value in the market and ensure that you receive a fair and equitable reward.

◆ Unless you share values with other people or are willing to accept their values, any relationship will be short-lived.

◆ You achieve a compound or collaborative relationship through two key behaviours: you must be able to find out and understand what success is for others; you must have the courage to advocate your needs so they understand what success is for you.

◆ A combination of the ability to give your needs and get the other person's wishes from them can result in four types of success: squandered; subordinate; selfish; and shared.

your choice now...

Remember that to change your mind and follow him who sets you right is to be none the less free than you were before.

Marcus Aurelius

Now you have a good understanding of the personal leadership framework, take a few minutes to map your current style against the following series of questions.

In-security

False ——————————————————————————— True

I feel secure in my ability to take action without the need for formal badges of office or power labels.

Choose your choice

False ——————————————————————————— True

I am able to push the pause button and prevent negative feelings or thoughts from being translated into inappropriate behaviour.

I manage my relationship on the principle of shared rather than selfish choice.

Know where you're going

I have a clear purpose and direction in my life that isn't decided by anyone else and sets out those things in life I will do and those that I will not.

I am confident that all my personal goals are achievable.

Rich variety

I always try to find new ways of looking at life so as to generate different ideas, thoughts and solutions.

Map your map

I never believe that my current view of the world is the truth, and accept that there are many ways of looking at one situation.

False ├──┼──┼──┼──┼──┼──┼──┤ True

I always try to view conflict in a relationship as a difference in our universes rather than a problem in the relationships.

Change how you change

False ├──┼──┼──┼──┼──┼──┼──┤ True

I manage change on the basis that it is a holistic process and can't be separated into discrete levels.

I manage change through a variety of styles using a refereed approach.

Thick trust

I invest time and energy in building thick trust funds with all people who are important to me.

Step inside out

False |—+—+—+—+—+—+—+—+—| True

I always present and frame the outcomes I need to achieve in a language and style that makes sense to others.

False |—+—+—+—+—+—+—+—+—| True

In any relationship I always try to see the world as others see it.

Share success

False |—+—+—+—+—+—+—+—+—| True

I achieve success in my relationships by helping others to know what I want and by understanding what they want.

False |—+—+—+—+—+—+—+—+—| True

I achieve success in my relationships by sharing my values, showing consideration for other people and appreciating the value of others.

Look back over the results you have given yourself. Think of one aspect that you'd most like to improve and where you believe you can realize a change in your personal leadership style. Try to crystallize the improvement you will make and write it in the box below.

The improvement I will make is:

_____

_____

_____

_____

_____

_____

_____

_____

_____

Now try to map this chosen improvement through the personal leadership framework.

Decision	Yes	Maybe	No
In-security. Are you happy that you have sufficient inner strength to stick with this change and not buckle if others suggest it's of little value or that you won't be able to change your current style?			
Choose your choice. What deep personal feelings, thoughts, and behaviours will you have to adopt? Know where you're going. Do you know why you want to make the change and how it will make a difference in the long run to your personal value?			
Rich variety. Did you consider all the options for improvement or did you just pick the first one that came to mind? What other improvement might you choose instead of this one?			
Map your map. Is your decision to improve an area of your personal leadership based on solid facts or JUST a suspicion that something needs to be improved?			
Change how you change. How will you manage the improvement? What alternative change strategies might you employ to ensure that you realize the change?			
Thick trust. Who else will you need to deliver the improvement to? What is the level of your trust fund with them?			
Step inside out. Do you understand the motivation of those people who will be involved in your improvement and why they might or might not wish to support you in your change?			
Share success. Are you clear as to the success that the change will realize for you and all the other people involved in the improvement?			
Results			

After using the personal leadership framework to reflect on your proposed change, are you still sure that this is the correct option? If so, you have achieved a success that few people achieve. You have taken time to seriously reflect upon how you will enhance your personal leadership style. Now that you have a new map of what's possible you can start to build a serious improvement plan that will help you lead yourself and others more effectively.

epilogue

Oz, left to himself, smiled to think of his success in giving the Scarecrow and the Tin Woodman and the Lion exactly what they thought they wanted. 'How can I help being a humbug,' he said, 'when all these people make me do things that everybody knows can't be done? It was easy to make the Scarecrow and the Lion and the Woodman happy, because they imagined I could do anything.'

Wizard of Oz

Personal leadership is just that — leading yourself. Don't be sucked into a belief that someone else can create a leadership solution for you. If you get this far in the book and agree that the core principles that underpin the need for personal leadership are right for you, the next thing to do is put the book away for a month. Go away and think about how you lead yourself and others; how you'd like to lead yourself and others; and what you might need to do to enhance this process. Then you can start to define where you're heading and how you'll get there in a way that fits your own map.

I wish you well on your journey.

Please feel free to e-mail me on mick@wizoz.co.uk or log on to the website at www.wizoz.co.uk to let me know how you're doing or to share your thoughts and feelings about the personal leadership framework.

references

1 Jones, H., 'Rodent or a rat bag?', *Financial Times*, 2 May 2000.

2 Ridpath, M., *The Marketmaker*, Penguin, London, 1998, p.110.

3 Bailey, J., 'King of Karma predicts bright future', *Sunday Times*, 4 June 2000.

4 Battram, A. Navigating Complexity, The Industrial Society, 1996, p.104.

5 Bolman G. and T. Deal, *Reframing Organisations*, Jossey Bass, 1991, p.14.

6 Ross, D., 'A star on the horizon', *Independent*, 7 August 2000.

7 Senge, P et al, *The Dance of Change*, Doubleday, New York, 1999, p.5.

8 Buchanan, D. and D. Body, *The Expertise of the Change Agent*, Prentice-Hall, New York, 1992.

9 Zand, D., 'Trust and Managerial Problem Solving', *Administrative Science Quarterly*.

10 Meyerson, W. and S. Kramer, 'Trust and Temporary Groups', *Trust in Organisations*, p.184.

11 Murray, D., 'Ken orders transport chiefs out of the cars and on to the tube', *Evening Standard*, 6 August 2000.

12 Hiscock, J., 'Vinnie plays it for real', *Daily Telegraph*, 25 July 2000.

13 Sims H. and P. Lorenzi, *The New Leadership Paradigm*, Sage Publications, USA, 1992, p.272.

14 Watson, E., 'How one phone call made up for 40 years of classroom war', *The Mail On Sunday*, 6 August 2000.

index